CONTENTS

Preface

The Setting

1. Confrontation! 17

2. Let's Talk 25

3. Burning in the Bosom? 33

4. Video Shock 45

5. What Is the Truth? 65

6. Searching for Answers 91

7. The Real Jesus 101

Notes

Creeds of Christianity

LDS Support Documentation

PREFACE

No one could have anticipated the shock waves which would reverberate throughout the world of Mormonism at the publication of the book *The God Makers* and the release of the Jeremiah film by the same name. Released in early 1984, the pair had an impact never before experienced in the 150-year history of the LDS Church. It was an impact from which they would never quite recover.

Crowds backed up for blocks to attend early film showings, and caselots of the books went from the book tables as fast as workers could make change. *The God Makers* changed the way the world would view Mormonism. This scene was being repeated in over a thousand churches per month. The book hit the Christian Best Sellers list and stayed there through the next year and more.

LDS apologists began challenging the film at every showing, standing during the question-and-answer times only to discover they were defenseless against its charges and the research by its authors. Major news articles and follow-up letters to the editors appeared in newspapers wherever the film and book showed up. The LDS Church issued battle plans and sets of instructions for local priesthood groups to use in trying to undermine the impact. The more the controversy grew, the bigger the crowds at the film showings grew, and the books went out by the tens of thousands.

The Arizona Chapter of the National Conference of Christians and Jews (NCCJ), operating under very liberal leadership and with approximately a dozen Mormons on their review committee, condemned the film and book as scurrilous works. LDS periodicals such as *Sunstone* and *Dialogue, Journal of Mormon Thought* published articles attacking the book and film, yet not a single unanswerable charge was ever produced.

Those *God Maker* books that made their way into public libraries were almost all immediately stolen, and numerous works by individual apologists began to appear in private attempts to stop the impact. Many personal accusations and charges were made public which attempted to attack the integrity of the authors and those former Mormons involved in the film showings.

Eventually, under the covering of the church, Dr. Gilbert Scharffs of Salt Lake City wrote the book *The Truth About the God Makers*, which was broadly distributed by the LDS Church in an attempt to counter the effect of *The God Makers*. The blatantly slanted and poorly researched book had no effect on the power of *The God Makers*, except for the faithful few who could hold the Scharffs work to their bosom in total loyalty to the LDS Church.

By now hundreds of thousands of copies of *The God Makers* had been sold and untold lives had been changed. The work of *The God Makers* still affects the lives of those involved in Mormonism. It has truly become a benchmark document in understanding Mormonism.

It was the highlight of my own life to have been one of its authors. Having spent almost 20 years of my adult life involved in the heart of the LDS Church system prior to becoming a "new creature in Christ" in 1975, I knew the problems of Mormonism from the inside out.

As Mormons we called ourselves true Christians, although we really felt superior to those of the rest of Christianity because we had so many written supplements to the Bible. We had a living prophet and so much more revealed information. When I was a Mormon I believed, as did my LDS friends and our leaders, that the Christian churches were led by those who were in the employ of Satan. This story is an honest response to those charges. It is written from the Mormon perspective, from the eyes and hearts of a Mormon couple and their orthodox Christian neighbor as they are caught up in a small corner of this controversy.

This story, in novel form, is my adaptation of the video film *The Mormon Dilemma* (SAINTS ALIVE, P.O. Box 1076, Issaquah, WA 98027).

—Ed Decker

INTRODUCTION

In the very quiet town in California the worst fears of the Mormon community were realized: A local church had sponsored the showing of the film *The God Makers*.

There were newspaper and radio ads promoting the film, and the presence of one of the people who appeared in the film, Ed Decker (head of one of the leading anti-Mormon organizations, Saints Alive), created further controversy.

Needless to say, the showing provoked a lot of community uproar. Mormons vigorously called and complained to the local newspaper and local radio station for doing highly visible interviews with Ed Decker. Pastors of the sponsoring churches began receiving constant phone calls from the local Mormon community. The emotions were high in both the LDS and the evangelical Christian communities.

This story deals with one typical Mormon family caught up in the Mormon side of the experience. They were outraged by the controversy, considering it an immoral condemnation of their faith. Matters became even worse when they discovered that their next-door neighbor was a member of the "offending" church that sponsored the film showing. They were deeply hurt when it was determined that he actually attended the events surrounding this "attack" on their religious rights.

Ted and Lorri Lindsey

Ted and Lorri Lindsey are the ideal Mormon family. Happily married, they live with their four children in a community in California where the LDS Church has had a recent explosion in growth.

They are in their early thirties. Ted is a returned missionary. Lorri met and married him at Brigham Young

University. She did not complete college, but dropped out when she became pregnant with their first child. Both went through LDS Seminary while in high school and LDS Institute while at BYU.

Lorri was born and raised in rural Utah. Ted grew up in the same California town where they now live, leaving only for his mission and his studies at BYU. He returned home with his wife and two children to work in his family business. They both hold active "Temple recommends," although they attend irregularly, usually during Ward Temple visitation days. They both wear "garments" regularly. While they have never discussed it, there is something about the Temple about which Lorri just doesn't feel quite right.

Ted is a counselor to the Bishop in the local Ward and teaches a Sunday School class. Lorri is an officer in the Stake Primary and teaches cultural improvement classes in the Relief Society. The local talk is that Ted is on his way up in the Church.

They were married, while at BYU, in the Provo Temple. Both sets of parents, other family members, and her grandparents attended. Her family was among the early pioneers. His family converted to the LDS Church while he was just under five.

Both husband and wife were raised in the Church within its traditional boundaries. They did everything expected of them and represent the real backbone of the LDS Church. They are asked to speak at church often, and both give strong testimonies during most testimony meetings.

They are good citizens, good neighbors, and loving parents, and they have strong family ties. They live a comfortable, upper-middle-class lifestyle. Any LDS family would be thrilled to have their children end up looking just like Ted and Lorri.

The overall appearance of this family is one of real substance, the ideal result of living the LDS commandments and being surrounded by the LDS environment. They are the kind of Mormons against which the film *The God Makers* seems to be so brazenly hurled, with such destructive force. It is from their point of view that we must deal with *The God Makers*.

It is pretty easy to line up *The God Makers* against the Church leadership and some of its apologists or against the real fruit of Mormonism, which are the broken homes, the discouragement, and the spirit of failure found in the 75 percent of LDS members who have never made it to the Temple even the first time—or that other 12 to 15 percent who have lost their worthiness and cannot go back to the Temple without going through the steps of a Church-regulated repentance.

But this family isn't in that group and is actually an example of the intended results of living the LDS faith—results by which other Mormons are judged. The Lorris and Teds really do exist throughout the LDS Church, although they are the result of far more things going for them than just membership in the Church. Yet in a confrontation of this nature they will give 100 percent credit to the Church for everything they are and ever will be.

Jim Stamper

Jim is their next-door neighbor. Jim is in his mid-forties, with graying hair. A recent widower, he is a mild-spoken, quiet person who is more comfortable in slacks and a cardigan sweater than he is in a suit. Jim is an active Christian and attends the church that has sponsored the film and meetings.

He attended the film showing and meetings with an intent on learning more about his neighbors' religion, so that he might understand them a bit more. He had come away from some earlier discussions with the Lindseys a little confused and somewhat wary of their doctrine. Jim is soundly comfortable in the Lord, fully able to calmly present the Gospel to the lost.

1

CONFRONTATION!

◆

Religion is something personal and something sacred. For most of us, we live and let live. But every now and then we are faced with religious confrontation, and we need to explain the reason for the faith that lies within us. Sometimes the challenge seems to take on the form of religious persecution, but whatever name we give them, such challenges usually take place in some *other* city and to some *other* people. We read about it and talk about it, but what do we do when it comes to *our* town?

There is no day in a small town that is more satisfying than a warm, quiet sunny Sunday morning. Everything is in slow motion. The streets are free of the usual busy weekday hustle, and except for the irregular clusters of cars hurrying to and from the various church services, the avenues remain empty and the stores at rest.

The LDS Ward building looks just like every other Mormon Church, with its brick exterior, well-groomed lawn, and simple spire fitting the LDS mold right down to the lettering of the name. This form of style duplication is part of the inner core of Mormonism. It's part of the LDS comfort zone and is found in such things as Sunday School lessons, manuals, missionary lessons, and even dress codes.

As the people begin to pour out of the meeting, the Lindseys seem to be smiling and laughing as they walk to the car... but there is a troubled look on Lorri's face. At church they have been discussing an attack against their religion right here in town, and she is gravely disturbed. Her dark mood throughout that day and into the next week is one of somber reflection and anxiety.

Lorri's kitchen has all the charm and utility of a happy home and busy mother, but there is no doubt that Lorri is upset. She is holding a section of the local newspaper in one hand, using it as a baton, accentuating each point as she speaks to one of her church friends on the phone. At the same time she is trying her best to get dinner prepared.

"I'm so upset I can't stand it!" she cried into the phone. "How can these people call themselves Christian? Those vicious people are getting rich attacking our church!"

"How could they do this to people who live right next to them? Jim Stamper has lived next door to us for five years! That film is being shown in the church he goes to! I'm going over there and tell him a thing or two!"

As her friend responded over the phone, Lorri reached over and grabbed some salad dressing from the refrigerator, her face a study of frustration and building anger.

Lorri interrupted, "I know, I know! He's on the radio this afternoon. I called them and told the station manager that if that evil man Ed Decker goes on the air . . . me, too!"

"What will happen to us now?" she asked with a tremor of fear. "Ted said we should just ignore it." She impatiently tapped a mixing spoon against the side of a bowl as her telephone friend tried to comfort her.

"I know, I know, but the Church has been my whole life," she continued. "The Bishop said what? . . . Well, I . . . who in the Ward would go, anyway?"

With a sudden grim look, Lorri cried into the phone, "I gotta go! Joshua will never go to bed tonight if I don't get him up from his nap. Oh . . . what kind of future can the kids expect if the persecution is already like this? . . . Bye . . . you too! Call me if you hear anything new."

She stared at the phone as though it were still alive, still sharing her fears. "Ted will make this go away," she thought as she headed for the boys' room.

Dinner was ready and the surface of Lorri's life was back in order when she heard the familiar sound of Ted's car pulling into the drive. With a sigh of relief she hurried out to meet him. In the driveway, Lorri glared across the yard as she watched Jim

Stamper getting into his own car. She stood with her hand on her hip, ignoring Ted as he reached out to greet her.

"What is it, honey? You look like you're on the warpath," he smiled as he kissed her in that husband-who-just-got-home-from-work kind of kiss.

Lorri turned from her angry stare. "It's that filthy movie they're showing in Jim's church tonight! Don't you even care? The whole town is going to be there! Just why isn't the Church putting a stop to this?"

Ted breathed a deep sigh and with great concern answered, "Look, Lorri, we've already gone over this at church. It's not the job of the Church to fight this persecution; its job is to proclaim the Gospel, perfect the Saints, and redeem the dead. The Stake President said we shouldn't get in a squirting contest with skunks! Now let's go inside."

"I'm not putting it aside that easily," Lorri said as they stepped back into the kitchen. "There is one thing we are going to do, and you can mark it under the section called 'Perfecting of the Saints,' " she exclaimed. "There is one next-door neighbor who is going to hear from one very angry Mormon lady! I hope his church believes in the laying on of hands!"

Both laughed and Ted pulled her close to him. "Okay," he smiled, "I'll be there to referee."

Then Ted turned serious. "I'm not minimizing this, Lorri. The Church is facing a lot of controversy from antagonists all over the world. It's just hard when it's going on right here in our own town, on our street. Remember, the Scripture says to 'pray

for them who spitefully use you.' But let's not let
these people ruin the rest of the evening for us.
Tomorrow is Saturday, and then we *will* go over and
have a talk with Jim."

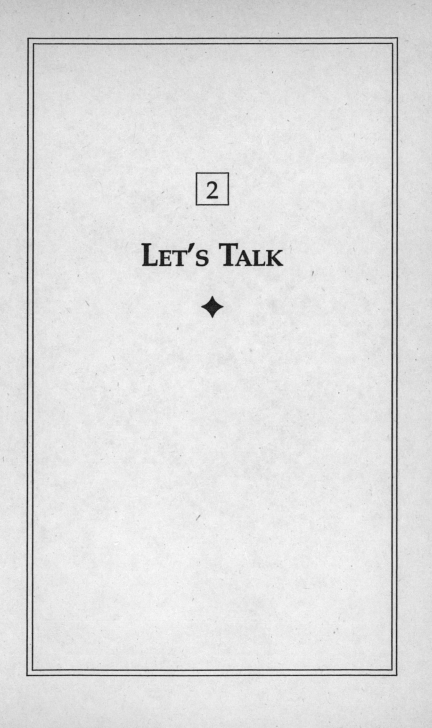

2

LET'S TALK

◆

J im Stamper worked with concentration, intent upon dismantling a well-bent lawn sprinkler head. He didn't see Lorri and Ted somewhat awkwardly approaching him until they were standing a few feet from him. Lorri's grim composure, her face reddened with a combination of both anger and fear, was far from her usual countenance.

Jim, looked up with a broad smile as they approached. "Hi, guys! Just fixing this sprinkler head I creamed with the car last week."

His smile turned to concern as he saw the anger in Lorri's face. "Lorri, is something wrong? What's the matter, Ted?"

Her face wrinkled with hostility, she scuffed her shoe in the grass as she cried out, "How could you?

Just how could you do that to us?" Everything seemed to be exploding in Lorri's head. She felt dizzy as she struggled to fight the tears, clinging tightly to Ted.

Jim took a deep breath and asked, "How could I do what to you?"

Ted responded in a controlled voice, his face taut and reddened: "How could you bring in those apostates and all their lies?"

"What kind of Christians are you, anyway?" Lorri added, giving Jim a scathing look.

Jim stepped back a few steps and looked curiously from Lorri to Ted. "Wait a minute. You're talking about that film last night, aren't you?"

Both replied, "Of course we are!"

"What did you think we would be talking about?" Lorri snapped. "That film is no better than this garbage," pointing to Jim's garbage can on the walkway.

Ted took Lorri by the hand and hushed her gently. "Jim, we thought you were our friend, and a good neighbor. I'm terribly disappointed that you would be involved with such an attack against our faith."

"First, I didn't order either the film or the speaker," Jim explained with some hesitancy. "It was done through the local ministerial group. It was only held at our church because we could handle a large crowd."

"Second, I went to see the film because even though you look and act like an ideal Christian couple, we don't speak on the same wavelength. I went to see the film so I could understand Mormonism better, and especially you two! I'm truly sorry if

I have offended you in any way, but I'm really glad I did see that film."

Lorri shook her head and stared at the ground before she looked up at her husband with an expectation of him responding.

"Jim, if you wanted to know about our church, we would have been overjoyed to share with you," he began. "We did try a few years ago, after Sally died, but you put us off pretty strongly. We're sorry, too."

Jim replied with a bit of a smile, "Well, I just wasn't ready to talk about eternal marriage to Sally by proxy. I just didn't understand what you really meant."

Ted brought the confrontation back to the film. "You know, don't you, that the film is filled with nothing but half-truths, misrepresentations of our doctrine, and outright lies!"

"It was done by excommunicated members of the Church," Lorri protested. "It's just filled with hate and error! They hate us so much they even mock our sacred ordinances."

"Have either of you seen the film," Jim asked?

As both vigorously shook their heads, Jim continued, "Well, I saw it and listened to an hour or more of some very tough questions afterward. It certainly has given me some new understanding of what is expected of you two."

Ted, offended, snapped back, "What do you mean by that remark?"

"Well, it's just that I have a deeper appreciation for the pressure that your beliefs put on you both. It makes me . . . well, anxious for you."

Lorri interrupted sharply, "You don't have to be anxious anymore, Jim Stamper! We can get along just fine without you worrying over us!"

Jim sighed, "I guess I'm not saying this right. I love you both. I want you to have the same joy in the Lord that I do. I just feel that . . . well, you'd have to see the movie to understand how burdened I am. I sure wish . . ."

Lorri broke in again, "I'd sooner die than walk into a church filled with people and have to sit there while some vile movie destroys what I believe is holy!"

Jim looked at the young couple with great concern, "Ted, Lorri . . . I have a lot of questions that need answering, and you could confront this thing privately. I can get a video of the movie and we could watch it together and you could help me to get a balanced picture of the real differences between Mormonism and my own faith. What do you say? For the sake of our common property line, we should be talking this problem out."

Ted responded, "There is no way my wife and I could sit through an hour of listening to ex-Mormons lie about us."

"Look. I understand exactly how you feel," Jim replied. "Let's do this. There's an eight- or ten-minute animation portion of the film that . . . at least, I think it portrays the very basic LDS theology. How about if I cue the video to that and we only watch that section? Then we can play it back piece by piece and you guys can straighten me out on it. It will certainly put an end to any problem of misunderstanding between us." He smiled broadly and waited as Ted and Lorri looked at each other.

"Let's do it, Ted," she said nervously. "We have the truth and we can watch at least one friend see it stand up against those lies. Let's do it once and for all!"

Ted nodded and turned to Jim. "Okay, you've got a deal. But remember we aren't going to sit there and have you knock our church while we don't argue with you. We *will* show you what we believe and why Heavenly Father would have us believe that way. *You can take it or leave it.*"

"I wouldn't want it any other way," Jim replied, smiling with obvious relief. "I'll be over tonight!"

Lorri tried smiling back with a grin that didn't match her voice. "Just come after 8:30. I want the kids in bed so there's no distraction." She turned quickly and walked off, Ted following behind. She was glad the confrontation was over but wary of the events to come.

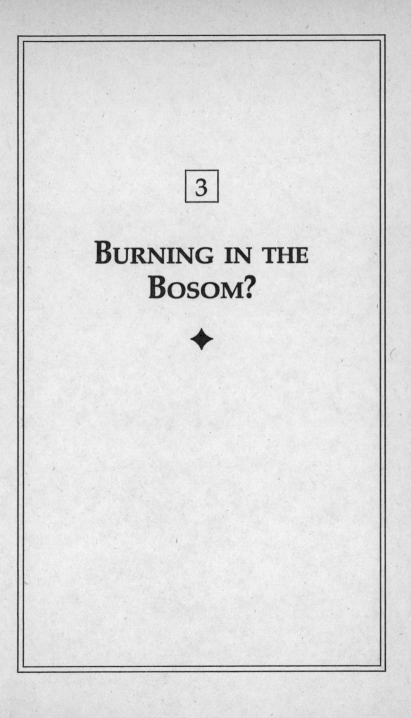

3

BURNING IN THE BOSOM?

✦

J im stood silently for several long minutes, watching as Lorri and Ted hurried up their drive and into the house. His thoughts drifted back to that day when his wife was taken to the hospital for the last time. He remembered looking back through the rear window of the ambulance as he anxiously held Sally by the hand.

Both Lorri and Ted had been standing at the foot of their driveway, watching as they pulled away from the house. Jim remembered thinking how odd it was that Lorri was smiling with a sort of "isn't that nice" kind of a smile. It was a smile that *still* stayed with him.

It was the beginning of the end for Sally, and as they prepared together for her imminent death, Jim was daily reminded of that smile as Lorri would go out of her way to greet him with a solicitous entreaty to wait until things were back to normal, when she and Ted would share some things of great importance to him and Sally. He realized even then that they were waiting until after Sally died to spring their plan for "eternal Marriage" upon him.

It was a pressure, an intrusion that began from the day of the funeral and lasted for almost a year. He finally blew up one day and ordered them from his home. This confrontation today was the first real conversation they had had since that time.

"Sally would never have listened to that for a minute," he reflected to no one in general but to the sprinkler head in specific. She placed her eternal faith in the Lord Jesus Christ. From the day he met her until that moment when she slipped away from him to be with Christ, Sally never wavered from the foundation of her faith.

Jim looked back at his neighbors' house. He shook his head as though he were trying to shake away the thoughts of the pain and emptiness he felt as he struggled to adjust to life without Sally at his side.

"I've set myself a real mess to deal with," he thought. "I think I better get myself down to the church, pick up a videocopy of the film, and have a talk with the pastor about this little visit tonight." Leaving the sprinkler head for a better day, Jim gathered up his tools and ambled back to his garage.

An hour later Jim was anxiously sharing his dilemma with his pastor. "They are *really* ready to take a piece out of me tonight, Tom," he exclaimed, waving his arms at the walls in the pastor's study in an unconscious effort to dramatize this increasing apprehension he was feeling. "I felt pretty confident this morning. I was in control of my emotions and really felt a tremendous love for them. But, boy, I'm not sure what I feel right now! It's like I'm mad at them for putting me in this position with their strange doctrine and mad at myself for not just leaving them alone with it."

Tom had been Jim's pastor and friend from even before that day when Jim, with great determination, walked down the center aisle of the church and surrendered his life to Jesus. As long as he could recall during this friendship, Tom knew Jim to be a caring, loving person. He was never one to be upset like this.

"Jim, you're suffering from the witnessing jitters," Tom smiled. "But in this case your neighbors have dumped a little guilt on top. Whenever you get this frustrated, you are either out of the Lord's will or just plain scared. What do you think is going on, Jim?"

Jim's gaze softened as he answered, "I know it's God's will that these two people and their family be saved. I know that their church's doctrine is far from orthodox and downright dangerous. Yet I'm not sure I'm ready to declare war on them. What I really need is some good advice on how to be an effective witness to Lorri and Ted. I want them to know what I know about Mormonism, Tom, and I want them to experience the joy of a true relationship with Christ. I guess I'm just plain scared that I can't do it."

Tom rose from his chair and came around the desk. He sat in the second of the two visitors' chairs and reached out, warmly thumping Jim on the arm.

The friends smiled at each other and Tom leaned back.

"I never knew *scared* was in your vocabulary, Jim," he laughed. "I'm pretty certain that you're solidly in God's will in this matter, and I'm equally convinced that you could give classes to the rest of us on sharing Christ—with anyone, anywhere!"

"I *do* think you need to review your motives, however. I think you need to be a real friend to this couple. There are a lot of spiritual scalp hunters out there who would love to win a Mormon soul for Jesus, but are completely unaware of the person who is that soul. You need to have an honest relationship with your Mormon friends before you try to witness. I'm sure you do, but how do you feel about it, Jim?"

Jim leaned forward and sighed deeply, "I *have* prayed about my own motives, and I think my association with Ted and Lorri is a real one. The last thing I want to do is argue theology with these folks! After I get past the simplicity of the real Gospel, what's left for me to even discuss, except respond to their theological variations?"

The pastor nodded as he replied, "It isn't quite that simple. Remember, your neighbors have been taught that they will be committing spiritual treason if they even *consider* your claims of the simplicity of the Gospel. Even so, you need to present it to them so that they *will* hear it. Again, I've got to go back to motive and how they perceive your witness. Is it from a friend of theirs or an enemy of their Church? You are in tough territory wherever you stand."

Jim thought for a moment and smiled. "Well, I guess it's up to me to show them I'm not their enemy. But after seeing the movie last night, I'm truly burdened for their souls. Somehow I just have to challenge them to listen to me. Somewhere tonight I have to find the key to reaching them."

"It has to be human interaction that makes the difference," Tom replied. "It has to be the kind of intensive, person-to-person witness through which Mormons are being won to Christ, Jim. There is no other way. As in every other kind of witnessing situation, what you *are* usually speaks louder than what you *say*!

"Then too, maybe you need to *listen* as much as you want to talk," Tom continued. "I'll bet that for every Mormon there is a different reason for being a Mormon and a different key to unlocking that mystery. Listen to them, Jim, until they're ready to listen to you. Don't jump at the first Mormon challenge to orthodoxy, no matter how tempting it is, until they have shared fully from their hearts."

He paused and then continued softly to his friend, "You have to love those two right now, just the way they are—unsaved, upset, angry Mormon neighbors. In no way can you let them come to the understanding that you only care for them as long as you might convert them. Remember, they're going to be looking to convert you, too!"

Jim raised his hand to interrupt. "I know I have to find some opening to share my own testimony of Christ, but how do you go about trading testimonies with people who use them as their stock and trade? It's their *burning in the bosom* that they use as their final evidence."

"You can't shy away from your own testimony just because they misuse the process," responded Tom. "A good place to begin is to tell them specifically how God has answered prayer in your life, how the Lord has changed you personally. But I suggest that you be careful in talking about the peace and joy you have in the Lord, no matter how true that is."

"Remember, those who follow Eastern religions or any number of the new cults will give such a testimony, as well as many happy Mormons, including your friends! Comparing burning bosoms isn't going to lead anyone to the Lord. Yet your testimony needs to emphasize that Christ is the sinbearer for Mormon and Gentile *alike*, and that they don't have to relinquish their Mormon heritage to accept Jesus."

Jim leaned back and smiled. "You're right! Their testimonies have always been centered around how much the Church has done for them, their marriage, their family, and their peace. They don't understand that it's *Christ* who does the changing of the natural man to the spiritual."

"I need to speak about those things the LDS Church can't deal with," Jim continued eagerly— "the power of the shed blood of Jesus, the cross and the nature of salvation by grace. I need to give them a good, clear definition of the doctrine of the Trinity.

"One other thing, Jim," Pastor Tom rejoined. "Tonight when the pressure is on, remember to answer their questions and objections from Scripture. But remember, you don't have to answer *every* question when it is asked. Don't try to bluff your way through *anything*! You can say, 'I don't know the answer to that, but I'll find out' or 'Let me think about it a little more and I'll give you an answer the next time I see you.' Then *find* the answer, be sure you understand it, and bring it back!"

"You don't have to remind me to bring my Bible with me tonight," Jim returned with a wave of his hand. "And I'm not going to let them concentrate only on the LDS/Christian proof texts. That's the ground where the Mormons are familiar, where they are prepared and trained for challenge. I learned that when they tried to convert me the last time. There is power in all the Scripture!"

Jim rose slowly from his chair. "I guess I'm as ready as I'll ever be, Tom. It's really been helpful to talk the whole thing through with you, and I've been praying it through ever since this morning. I just ask your prayers on their behalf as I meet with them tonight."

The pastor rose and placed his hand on Jim's shoulder with unmistakable affection and concern. "I'll do better than that! We'll get the church prayer team on this before you even reach your car!"

Jim could see the deep commitment in the eyes of his pastor, and it strengthened him. "You don't know how much your prayer support has always meant to me, Tom. Maybe the whole reason for this Mormon film and speaker last night was to bring the situation next door to the point that I can share the truth with Ted and Lorri. I'm really confident that it will be okay tonight!"

Tom smiled and said quietly, "Jim, let's go over the basics here about prayer. *Always* pray before any visit like tonight. Going into this sphere of spiritual contact without the Holy Spirit is dangerous to both you and your Mormon friends. The Scripture promises us the power of the Holy Spirit to guide and direct us at times such as this. *Always* ask the intervention of the Holy Spirit to draw the Mormon to the cross of Jesus for salvation.

"Realize also that the Mormon is under spiritual bondage which can only be lifted through intercessory prayer, from committed people like you and our prayer team. If you have a burden for this couple, it's vital that you be involved in persistent, aggressive prayer directed against the principalities and powers of Mormonism.

"Pray according to the Bible that the strong man be bound so that the captives can be set free. Ask God to pull down the strongholds of Mormonism and cast down vain imaginations and 'every high thing that exalts itself against the knowledge of God.' "

Tom grinned broadly as he continued, "Those are heavy instructions, but you're a warrior, Jim! Mormonism's bondage and power over this couple can be broken through prayer in the name of Jesus. They won't be the first ones who have been set free through the intercession of committed Christian friends and they won't be the last! Let's take a few minutes and pray right now."

Burning in the Bosom?

The two men knelt at the chairs. With a sigh, Jim began to cry out to the Lord as tears welled up in his eyes, "O Lord, make me an instrument of Your salvation."

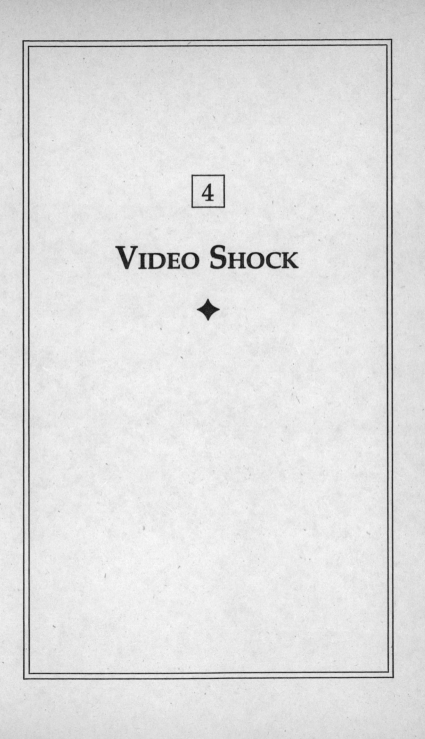

4

VIDEO SHOCK

✦

T ed and Jim were sitting in front of the Lindsey TV as Lorri walked in hurriedly from the hallway.

"Okay! The last of the litter is all tucked away," she laughed nervously as she sat down on the sofa next to Ted. "I'm sorry to keep you waiting so long."

Both men smiled as Ted hugged her, "That's okay, honey. Sit down and let's see just what has everybody in such an uproar. I'm just glad I didn't have to do the bedtime job tonight."

"I have the video all set to go, if you two are ready to begin," Jim said with some hesitation. With their quick nods, he clicked the remote and the first scenes of the animation portion of *The God Makers* filled the room.

They were the longest few minutes Jim had ever

experienced. It was obvious that the screen held both Ted and Lorri in rapt attention. He was certain that there was a mounting fury building in his two Mormon friends.

The video ended with stone silence. Both Lorri and Ted stared at the TV as though too stunned to speak. Ted turned to look at Lorri, who continued her stare.

Lorri turned slowly to Jim , her face a hostile mask, and spoke in a tight, controlled voice. "Jim, that is the most demeaning, vicious piece of fantasy that I have ever seen. That cartoon has about 5 percent truth and 95 percent misrepresentation. Are you sure that it's the Mormon Church they're talking about?" she asked with biting sarcasm.

Ted was no happier over the situation "Well, I'm obviously appalled by it," he said to his friend. "They have a lot of LDS theology all thrown together with some real exaggerations and sensationalism. If I were a non-Mormon seeing that for my first look at the Church, I'd stone the first missionaries unfortunate enough to show up at my door."

"I'm *sure* that is *exactly* what they had in mind," Lorri responded.

Jim didn't have to be told that he was in dangerous waters. "I'm so sorry to be involved in such an offense to you," he sighed. "Well, at least we have a place to start. I'd like to go through it section by section and let you folks tell me what your church *really* teaches, what you both *really* believe!"

"I'm not sure if I can stomach another roll through that garbage again," Lorri snapped. "Babies with diapers in the preexistence!"

But Ted was determined. "I'm game, Jim. That film is a genuine danger to our faith. At least we can set one misled friend straight."

"Look, if what you say is true," Jim said hopefully, "I can promise that I'll be at my pastor's door before he even gets out of bed tomorrow. I want the truth every bit as much as you do!"

Ted's mind was now ready to put these lies to the test. "Rewind that thing and let's get at it. Honey, could you run in the study and bring out the Scriptures? And get *Mormon Doctrine*, too. Wait! I'll go with you," he said as he jumped up with Lorri. "There are a few other things I think will be helpful too."

As Ted and Lorri left the room, Jim rewound the video. He was just finishing as Ted and Lorri returned with a pile of books and looks of strong determination. Lorri held out a large white book and showed Jim the cover.

"I found our *Temple Preparation Manual* too. It covers a lot of the same subject, but it was prepared to bless people, not curse them," she said with a dry laugh. "It's what we really believe, not a bunch of lies!"

"Okay, honey," Ted interjected. "Jim isn't our enemy; he's our friend. Let's not let our anger at those people spill over onto him."

"Well, I'm not sure he isn't," she growled back.

"I'm not your enemy, guys. I really am your friend, Lorri," Jim hurried to reply. "What you watched is the eight-minute illustrated section from the movie *The God Makers*. Let's go back to the start and take it step by step."

"What a title," Lorri muttered sarcastically.

Jim quickly hit the remote. "Okay, now I'm going to play just a bit into the animation. I'll stop it when we get to the first break."

Their attention turned to the television as the video began playing the actual animation. *"Mormonism teaches that trillions of planets scattered throughout the cosmos are ruled by countless gods who once were human like us."*

Jim hit the pause button and turned to the Lindseys. "Now, is that true?"

"Well, we actually do believe that we aren't God's only creation," Ted answered thoughtfully. "We do believe that there are countless planets in the universe where children of God, like us, are working out their salvation or have worked out their salvation and gone on."

"The word 'trillion' bothers me," added Lorri. "But we *do* have a saying in the Church that I think will help you understand where we're coming from. Lorenzo Snow said it a long time ago: 'As man is, God once was; and as God is, man may become.' It's called the Law of Eternal Progression."

"Okay, then. That kind of explains this next part," Jim responded.

"They say that long ago, on one of these planets, to an unidentified god and one of his goddess wives, a spirit child named Elohim was conceived. This spirit child was later born to human parents who gave him a physical body."

Lorri began leafing through the Temple Manual as Ted frowned. "Okay, let's get that statement desensationalized. We *do* believe that we were spirit children of our Father in Heaven—we call it the

Preexistence. You know, God told Jeremiah He knew him before He formed him in the womb. He said He even called him and ordained him to be a prophet before he was born! How did He know him before he was born? He knew him in the Preexistence."[1]

Ted lifted a heavy black book and continued, "One of our apostles, Bruce R. McConkie—in this book, *Mormon Doctrine*—says God had a father, and he says that *He* also had a father."[2]

"You mean *God* had a grandfather?"

"Well, I guess you could say that."

Lorri handed the Temple Manual to Ted and gave Jim the first real smile of the evening, "It says right here that Elohim once lived on an earth like ours."[3]

"And this is what you call The Law of Eternal Progression?" Jim asked.

"Yes. *The Pearl of Great Price* says everything is made spiritually before it is made physically.[4] That goes for people, too."

"*Through obedience to Mormon teaching, death, and resurrection, he proved himself worthy and was elevated to godhood as his father before him.*"

Lorri picked up the manual again and turned toward Jim. "In our Temple Preparation Manual it says that God became God through obedience to the Gospel program[5]—I doubt that they called it Mormonism, though. Mormon was a prophet who lived here on this earth and kept the record of the people in the Americas. The Church got its nickname from the Book of Mormon, named after him. There is a whole section in the manual that talks about this."

"Okay, then let's get the rest of this subject out," Jim said with a frown.

"Mormons believe that Elohim is their Heavenly Father and that he lives with his many wives on a planet near a mysterious star called Kolob. Here the god of Mormonism and his wives, through endless Celestial sex, produced billions of spirit children—"

"Let's stop right here!" Lorri protested. "I don't *believe* that Elohim is my Heavenly Father, I *know* he is. Endless sex, millions of wives, and billions of children all running around on a mysterious star is what drives me crazy!"

Ted took the manual from his wife and pointed it at Jim. "The film ridicules us, but we do believe that God procreated us as spirit children. Lorri and I went through the Temple Preparation classes together. Listen to this. It says: '. . . God is an exalted man who once lived on an earth and underwent experiences of mortality. . . . His marriage partner is our mother in heaven. We are their spirit children, born to them in the bonds of Celestial marriage.' "[6]

Looking up from the pages, he continued, "I guess if that's what you want to call 'endless Celestial sex,' so be it! And, yes, we—without apology—believe we have a high destiny, even Godhood. Let me read just one other thing: '. . . and you have got to learn to become Gods yourselves, and to be kings and priests to God, the same as all Gods have done before you.' That's the Prophet Joseph Smith speaking, sharing truth that Christianity has long since forgotten!"[7]

"Lorri," Jim asked, keeping his voice soft, "Have

all the people born in this world first been conceived as spirit children—been fathered by Elohim?"

"Of course!"

"Then doesn't it stand to reason that there must
be at least more than a billion spirit children? You
didn't like that term 'billion,' but look at the world
population and the number of people who have
already lived and died. I was wondering, Ted—is
polygamy a possibility here?"

"Yes, you're right. It does seem probable. The
Doctrine & Covenants does imply that we may have
the opportunity to have plural wives in the Celestial
Kingdom—the Scripture that directed Joseph Smith
and Brigham Young to take more than one wife is
still in my *D&C*."[8]

*"To decide their destiny, the head of the Mormon gods
called a great heavenly council meeting. Both of Elohim's
eldest sons were there, Lucifer and his brother Jesus."*

"The *Book of Abraham*, in the *Pearl of Great Price*,
says that God called a council of all the leading
spirits.[9] Joseph Smith said that the 'Head of the
Gods called a council of the Gods'—I'm sure that's
where they get that. My Priesthood Manual says
that Joseph Smith was at that council as one of the
choice spirits."[10]

"What about the part about Jesus and Lucifer?"
Jim burst out. "Are they literally brothers?"

"We were *all* brothers and sisters in the Preexistence," Lorri smiled at him. "Play the next part. You
have to understand about what the council did.
Until that time Lucifer was equal to Jesus."

"A plan was presented to build planet Earth where the spirit children would be sent to take on mortal bodies and learn good from evil. Lucifer stood and made his bid for becoming savior of this new world. Wanting the glory for himself, he planned to force everyone to become gods. Opposing the idea, the Mormon Jesus suggested giving man his freedom of choice as on other planets. The vote that followed approved the proposal of the Mormon Jesus who would become savior of the planet Earth."

"You see!" Lorri exclaimed, "Lucifer wanted the glory that belonged to Heavenly Father!"

Jim's face melted into astonishment. He looked at them incredulously as he asked, "Then this *really is* what actually happened?"

"The words are fine," Ted said while still staring tightly at the screen. "It's the science-fiction photography I object to," he added with a measured voice. "Go ahead, I'm waiting for something in the next section."

"Enraged, Lucifer cunningly convinced one-third of the spirits destined for earth to fight with him and revolt. Thus Lucifer became the devil and his followers the demons. Sent to this world, they would forever be denied bodies of flesh and bone. Those who remained neutral in the battle were cursed to be born with black skin. This is the Mormon explanation for the Negro race. The spirits that fought most valiantly against Lucifer would be born into Mormon families on planet Earth. These would be the lighter-skinned people, or 'white and delightsome,' as the Book of Mormon describes them."

Lorri stared at him. "I'm sorry, Jim, but that bit with people turning into demons and turning black is just sick!"

"It's not only sick, it's terribly inaccurate," Ted responded confidently. "First, there were no neutrals in the battle. Those who rebelled were cast from God's presence and sent to this earth without bodies, although I doubt they went the way the cartoon shows us. Today, these same demons continue to battle against the Saints. The *Book of Abraham*, the *Book of Moses*, and the *Doctrine and Covenants*, all give a clear picture of the whole thing.[11]

"The filmmakers are trying to show that the LDS Church is racist, which is the farthest thing from the truth. Blacks have always been able to be members of our church. The Lord forgave them any preexistence punishment in 1978, and now they too can hold the priesthood—which actually was the *real* punishment, not the skin color. And now blacks *can* marry in the temple.

"The Scriptures in *Moses*[12] explain it. Bruce R. McConkie said their skin was marked through the lineage of Cain. It was so they could be recognized as those who couldn't hold the priesthood. But fortunately all of that has now changed."[13]

Lorri felt on solid ground and confided, "The Temple Manual *does* say that the choicest spirits are now coming to earth to LDS families."[14]

"Doesn't it bother you a little that millions of blacks died with that curse?" Jim shot back.

"Of course not," she answered with a shrug. "Heavenly Father loves them. They will get a chance in Spirit Prison to accept the Gospel and the Priesthood. That's why baptism for the dead is *so* important."

"Okay, well, let's wait till we get there. I'll go to the next section if it's okay with you two." Lorri and Ted nodded in agreement.

"Early Mormon prophets taught that Elohim and one of his goddess wives came to the earth as Adam and Eve to start the human race. Thousands of years later, Elohim in human form once again journeyed to earth from the star base Kolob, this time to have physical relations with the Virgin Mary in order to provide Jesus with a physical body."

Ted became gravely serious. "Again, the whole presentation is totally without taste and it's meant to offend. The Church no longer accepts the Adam-God Theory, even if Brigham Young did believe it. It's just in there to sensationalize again.

"And regarding the physical conception of Jesus," he continued, "you just have to take it out of the gutter and put it into eternal perspective. *Mormon Doctrine* again clears it up. It says that Jesus was begotten by an immortal father in the same way that mortal fathers beget children. Jesus was conceived and born in the *normal* and *natural* way.[15] What's so *strange* about that, Jim?"

"I'm sorry, but I have always believed in the virgin birth. This is far from orthodox theology. Do you agree with Ted, Lorri?"

"We *do* believe in the virgin birth," she emphasized. "Mary was certainly a virgin *before* she was overshadowed by Heavenly Father. I know some people believe Jesus was conceived by the Holy Ghost, but the Holy Ghost is a completely different personage and is still a spirit being and is probably incapable of fathering a physical child. We studied this in our Gospel Doctrine class, didn't we, Ted?"

"Yes, we did," he assured her. "At least five General Authorities, including three *presidents* of the Church, have taught clearly that Jesus was conceived through natural relations between God the Father and the Virgin Mary."

"By 'natural relations,' you mean sexual intercourse?" Jim asked, smiling faintly.

"Call it what you like!" she shot back.

Ted sat at the edge of his seat, concern written across his face. "This whole conversation is a little speculative, like the idea that Jesus was a polygamist."

"That's coming up," Jim replied. "Let's look at it."

"Mormon Apostle Orson Hyde taught that after Jesus Christ grew to manhood, he took at least three wives— Mary, Martha, and Mary Magdalene. Through these wives the Mormon Jesus supposedly fathered a number of children before he was crucified. Mormon founder Joseph Smith is supposedly one of his descendants."

Ted smiled thinly. These were areas not usually discussed with investigators, and for good reason. "That whole section is *apostate doctrine*," he said with authority. "None of that is currently taught by any authority in the Church. I do know from my BYU studies that Joseph Smith, through *personal revelation*, told several of the early leaders that they were descendants of Jesus. The rest comes from old speeches in the *Journal of Discourses* which we don't accept as doctrinal today. This section is in the film just to make us look strange."

"But if Joseph Smith and Apostle Hyde *taught* it," Jim protested, "then—"

Lorri broke in, "Well, personally, I *believe* it. If Joseph Smith taught it, then it's true! Besides, it makes sense. If God commanded polygamy for early Church members, if God is married in heaven, if—"

"Yes, but this is exactly where we get into trouble," Ted scowled. "Frankly, I'm not into speculation. And I don't really care *what* early Church leaders taught. I'm interested in what the Church teaches *today*. When everybody was upset over the blacks and the priesthood revelation, Bruce R. McConkie said—quote—'It doesn't make a particle of difference what *anybody* said prior to June First, 1978—it's a new day and a new arrangement.'[16]

"This whole line of discussion is out of order," he murmured as his face reddened. "Our General Authorities deserve better from us, Lorri."

Flustered, Lorri began, "But, Ted, dear, I just felt that . . ." A look into his eyes told her to stop. She forced a smile, trying to stop the fear inside.

Jim was having a bit of a struggle. "Well, I'm more than a little uncomfortable with that kind of blind obedience . . ." Looking at the couple, he knew he was on dangerous ground, and his voice trailed to a stop. Pushing himself back into the chair, he turned to the television. "But, okay, let's not dwell on it, then. I'm anxious to get into the Book of Mormon material."

"According to the Book of Mormon, after his resurrection Jesus came to the Americas to preach to the Indians, who the Mormons believe are really Israelites. Thus the

Jesus of Mormonism established his church in the Americas as he had in Palestine. By the year 421 A.D., the dark-skinned Israelites, known as the Lamanites, had destroyed all of the white-skinned Nephites in a number of great battles. The Nephites' records were supposedly written on golden plates buried by Moroni, the last living Nephite, in the Hill Cummorah."

Ted perked up and grinned, "Well, this is pretty straight information. We believe that the people in the Americas were the 'other sheep' who were mentioned by Jesus in the New Testament."

Lorri began to smile. "That's the kind of thing you can only get from reading the Book of Mormon and praying. Moroni 10:4 says that if you pray with a sincere heart and real intent, having faith in Christ, he will manifest it to you by the Holy Ghost," she told Jim brightly. "You will get a burning in the bosom and *know* it's true. Even though I was raised in the Church, I didn't get my own testimony until I went away to college. I *know* the Book of Mormon is the Word of God and I *know* that Joseph Smith was a true Prophet of God. I bear you my testimony that I *know* the Church of Jesus Christ of Latter-day Saints is the Only True Church."

Jim studied her smiling face, and with a voice softened by extreme caution he replied, "I'm sure you do know that, Lorri. I can see how important these things are to you."

Ted saw the same danger point in Lorri's still-frozen smile. "We have some really bad stuff coming up about Joseph Smith that upsets me. Let's continue," he directed. *Maybe this wasn't the wisest thing to put Lorri through*, he reflected as the video began.

"1400 years later a young treasure-seeker named Joseph Smith, who was known for his tall tales, claimed to have uncovered the same gold plates near his home in upstate New York. He is now honored by Mormons as a prophet because he claimed to have had visions from the spirit world in which he was commanded to organize the Mormon Church because all Christian creeds were an abomination. It was Joseph Smith who originated most of these peculiar doctrines which millions today believe to be true."

"This is pure character assassination," Ted groaned. "First, I know about his 'treasure-hunting'—everybody did it in those days. It was called 'folk magic.' Then they take a mother's offhand comment about a young son's storytelling and he becomes 'a teller of tall tales.' He didn't *claim* to find the plates, he *found* them and translated them by the gift and power of God.

"Three witnesses swore to it and later eight more honest men also testified that they saw them. Your 'visions from the spirit world' are called 'revelations' by those of us who are believers.

"He didn't originate these *peculiar* doctrines; it was Heavenly Father who originated these *true* doctrines! They were only peculiar because no church on the face of the earth was following them anymore. Their creeds were all abominations to God."[17]

"Ted's right," Lorri said easily. "We honor Joseph Smith just as much as we do Moses and Jeremiah and Peter and Paul, and Jesus. Joseph holds the keys to this dispensation just as they did in theirs. And Jim, how could a 15-year-old kid write the Book of

Mormon, anyway?" She was back on top, the mysterious ashen look of moments ago erased, her look one of vigor and determination.

"I understood that the Book of Mormon was not published until Joseph Smith was 25."

"Well, whatever," she answered. "But he was seeing visions when he was 14!"

"If it's okay with you both," Jim asked, "I'd like to get back to this after we finish the review, because I have a couple of questions that may take a little time, okay?" They nodded simultaneously.

"By maintaining a rigid code of financial and moral requirements, and through performing secret temple rituals for themselves and the dead, the Latter-day Saints hope to prove their worthiness and thus become gods. The Mormons teach that everyone must stand at the final judgment before Joseph Smith, the Mormon Jesus, and Elohim."

"What's wrong with being moral and paying tithes and supporting the work of God?" Lorri complained. "I'll bet your pastor would love to have a congregation like that!"

"Jim, what we do in the Temple is not *secret*, it's *sacred*. Lorri and I were married in the Provo Temple while we were at BYU. That was after I spent several years of my life serving my Church in the mission field.

"Jesus went to the temple and so did all those who wanted to be closer to God," Ted continued. "There is no difference in what we do today. We don't show movies about it because it's holy and you must be worthy to participate in its sacred ordinances. The Temple is the door to the Celestial Kingdom and eternal marriage."

"You have to have a Temple recommend," Lorri added.

"What about this business of Joseph Smith being your judge?"

"That's out of context, Jim. First, they purposely put it backward. It's Elohim, Jesus, and *then* Joseph.

"In my Priesthood Manual there is a whole section on it. I remember that we had quite a lively discussion about it in Priesthood meeting. But our Priesthood manual stated plainly that if we are to get our salvation, we shall have to pass by Joseph Smith. If we enter our glory, it will be through the authority that he has received. We can't get around him.

"Joseph Smith holds the keys to this dispensation—he is its head and will be throughout all eternity. Of *course* he will be at the judgment bar, but I can assure you that he is there as your friend to plead your case if need be. But nobody will go to the Celestial Kingdom without his express approval."[18]

"That's why it's so important that you accept Joseph Smith as a true Prophet. Jim, wouldn't it be great to be sealed to your wife and spend eternity with her? Right now you're only married to her until death do you part—*your marriage is over*. Our church offers hope to you that you can't have anywhere else. That's how important Joseph Smith's revelations are to you personally."

As they sat smiling broadly at him, Jim stared back without a word, his expression dark and rigid. After several moments of frozen silence he spoke in almost a whisper. "Let's continue." Turning with some deliberation, Jim flipped on the last section of video.

"Those Mormons who were sealed in the eternal marriage ceremony expect to become polygamous gods in the Celestial Kingdom, rule over other planets, and spawn new families throughout eternity. The Mormons thank God for Joseph Smith, who claimed that he had done more for us than any other man, including Jesus Christ. The Mormons claim that he died as a martyr and shed his blood for us so that we too may become Gods."

Ted jumped in as the video ended. "We have already been given a small picture of what heaven can be like. Lorri and I—and our children—will stay in the family unit through all eternity. That polygamy stuff is real, all right. But why is it all so evil? Abraham and his sons had more than one wife. So did Solomon, and probably so did the apostles! Why is it okay for them and not us?"

Lorri began reading from the Temple Manual: " 'If we keep our covenants and are faithful to the end, we shall come forth as gods and receive a fulness of the Kingdom.' Ted will be a King and a Priest and I will be his Queen and Priestess," she cried out, pointing to the text.[19]

"We thank God for Joseph Smith," Ted pronounced defiantly, "who has done more for us than any man, *save Jesus*—That's in *Doctrine and Covenants*, Section 135. And that is what the Church teaches."

Pointing to the TV, he added, "*They* are quoting from an obscure statement made by Joseph Smith in *The History of the Church*."[20]

Lorri stepped to the TV and switched it off. She was pleased and in control. "Look, guys, the video is over and we've been at this ordeal forever. Come on in the kitchen and have some punch and cookies."

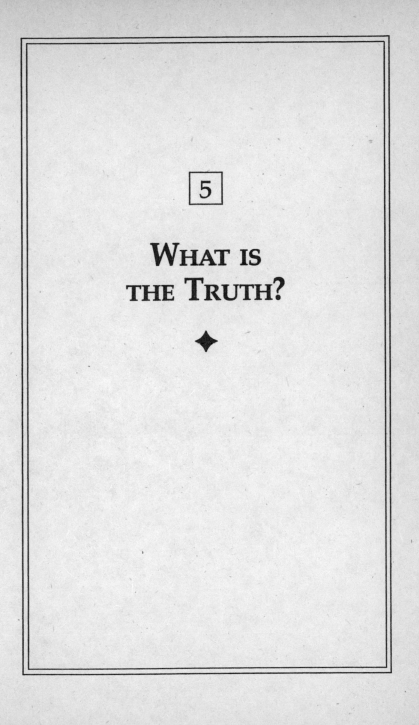

5

WHAT IS THE TRUTH?

◆

J im stretched as he stood. "Well, it's been a very interesting evening."

Ted reached over and put his hand on Jim's shoulder as they walked toward the kitchen. "We've been glad to tell you how we really feel, but I'm afraid we haven't really changed your mind much."

As a matter of fact, you haven't," Jim responded. "In fact, the things you said sort of confirmed what the film was saying—at least as far as I can tell."

"Except that the film takes everything out of context and distorts and exaggerates it."

Jim smiled as he said, "I'm sure both of us can't escape the fact that our backgrounds color how we view things. But I have to confess that I'm troubled as much by your explanation of your faith as I am by the film. I mean you can strip away all of the—in your words 'sensationalism'—and basically, you're telling me that Mormonism teaches some things that are very repugnant to me as a Christian."

Lorri stepped back in surprise. "Like what?"

Jim lowered himself slowly into a chair at the table. "Well, first, that men may become Gods!"

"I have to admit, that really *is* the bottom-line difference between our positions," Ted acknowledged. "As I see it, one of us is right and one of us is wrong."

Jim grinned broadly. "Well, we are in absolute agreement on one point, anyway."

"Now I know it's a strange concept when you first hear it," Ted continued, ignoring the joke, "but if it *is* true, it's one of the most important revelations ever to come to man."

"You're right—*if it is true*," Jim shot back. "On the other hand, if it is *not* true—in other words, if Joseph Smith *didn't* get that information from God— if men can *never* become Gods, then Mormonism is teaching something that is, well—*evil!*"

Ted glanced at Lorri before he replied. "I don't see it that way at all. If I'm wrong, I'm simply wrong. I've made a mistake. I'm still a Christian. I still believe in the Savior. I don't see why it's necessarily evil—not to mention that it's *true*.

Lorri joined in. "Why do we always have to be *evil* to you Christians? Whatever happened to live and let live?"

Jim ignored Lorri and continued to address Ted. "From my Christian perspective, the concept that men can become Gods is a very basic doctrinal error that leads men away from the true worship of God in pursuit of their own Godhood."

Ted felt comfortable with the question. His skills in dealing with these life-changing questions were sharpened during his mission for the church. He was on solid ground. "Yes, Jim, it may be hard for *you* to understand, but it is *God's* plan. We're to become like our Father in Heaven. Don't you remember the Scripture, 'Be ye perfect, even as your Father in Heaven is perfect?' "

Lorri leaned over the table as though to take Jim's hand. "And isn't it natural to want to be like Heavenly Father? After all, man *was* made in His image."

Jim leaned away from the table and the intensity of the two. "Okay, hold on. Back off and let me take this one step at a time. Yes, of course, I think it is my destiny to become perfect—when I go to heaven, that is. But I'm going to become a perfect *man*, not a God. One of the things you misunderstand is the basic difference between men and God—and for that matter, angels. You have men and angels and God all mixed up. They are—at least according to the Bible—three entirely different beings. A man can become a perfect man, if he is sinless; but he can no more become a God than a cat can become a dog."

Ted smiled as he replied, "That's *your* interpretation of what the Bible teaches!"

"All right," Jim conceded, "I think we can think this through rationally together. Do you mind if I tell you a little of my philosophy about the nature of God?"

"Of course not. I'd be delighted to hear what you think."

Jim leaned over into the center of the table, his eyes speaking to both of them. "One of the fundamental problems I see here is that Mormonism has failed to think its theology through to its rational end. What I mean is that Mormonism—if I have understood you correctly—teaches that Elohim was once a man. Is that right?"

"We have already said that he was."

"Okay, so Elohim was a man. But was *he born* as a 'spirit child' to another God?" Jim asked.

Lorri looked from Ted to Jim. "*That's* what we're trying to tell you!"

"That's what Orson Pratt and others taught," Ted added. "That's why we can expect to become Gods."

"Well, don't you see that there is a philosophical flaw in that thinking?" Jim probed.

"I certainly do not!" Ted shot back with vigor.

Jim took one of those long deep breaths and began, "Well, think about it. If a God has to have been a man to work his way to Godhood—then how did the first man come into existence? Who created *him*? According to your theology, no matter how you slice it, if Gods have to be men before they can become Gods, then the first man came into existence out of nothing, since there was no God to create him."

"And that's logically inconsistent. Rational thought dictates that a super intellect must exist at the beginning of creation. That super intellect is described as God. He is the Creator. Some call him the prime mover, or the first cause, or that being beyond which no greater can be imagined.

"Now if such a being had a father, he *can't* be that absolute God. His *father* might have been, but *he* isn't. As I see it, if you worship Elohim, then you are worshiping a being who is no greater than yourself may soon become."

Ted wondered just how much of the Mormon Gospel plan Jim was ready to absorb. "In a sense that's true. Joseph Smith said we were co-eternal with God," he responded softly.

Jim seemed confused. "Well which is it? If you are co-eternal with God, then you have existed as long as he has, which would do away with your having been procreated as a spirit child. That's what I mean when I say there is no satisfactory philosophical footing here. What you seem to have is a collection of speculations."

Lorri was getting that defensive look again. "And do you have something *better*?"

"I sure do!"

"Well, what is it?"

"The Bible," he answered softly.

"Your *interpretation* of the Bible, you mean," Ted quipped.

"No, I don't think so," he answered. "The Bible tells us very clearly about the nature of God. For 2000 years the definition has served the Christian church very well.

"Yeah, but *which* Christian Church?" Ted wanted to know. "There are hundreds of denominations."

"I take it that you assume all these denominations are in doctrinal disagreement," Jim replied.

"They certainly are!" Lorri interjected. "Why else would there be so many different churches? That's what Joseph Smith and the Book of Mormon is all about—to bring an end to that confusion."

Ted picked up the cue from his wife. "Joseph is the Prophet of the Restoration. Because of the apostasy of the Christian church, God sent Joseph to restore plain and precious truths which had been lost. Jim, don't you assume that God would have order in His church?"

Again Jim studied their faces before replying, "First, I assume *nothing* that the Bible doesn't teach clearly. There certainly *is* authority in God's church, but I see no evidence in the Bible for a monolithic, authoritarian church with a man at its head. Jesus, the Bible says, is the *only* Head of His church.

"Jesus said He would establish His church and the gates of hell would never prevail against it. Apparently you believe the gates of hell *did* prevail, so that the authority of God was lost from the earth and Joseph Smith had to restore it. Is that right?"

"Exactly," Ted smiled. "Well, maybe not quite exactly, but the authority *was* lost and had to be returned."

Jim relaxed a bit and returned the smile. "Look, the authority in the church of Christ is the Bible. I think this might surprise you, but the fact that there are denominations is evidence of the *health* of the Church, not of division."

"That sounds like double-talk," Lorri grumbled.

"Let me put it this way," Jim replied. "I go to the Christian Center. That's my church. But I'm a Christian first. I could be very happy going to a Baptist

Church or a Presbyterian Church or a Lutheran Church. For me, the church is bigger than the group that meets in my building. I get the impression that you think Baptists and Presbyterians and Methodists are somehow divided on basic Bible truth."

"Well, aren't they?" Ted challenged.

"Absolutely not. All of them subscribe to the authority of the Bible. On the important issues of the faith like the nature of God, the fall of man, the incarnation of Jesus, and the remedy for sin, they are absolutely united. These doctrines were hammered out early in the history of the church. In fact, the creeds, which you and Joseph Smith call abominable, articulate those basic doctrines and are received by all Bible-believing Christians." (See Appendices.)

"Then why have denominations at all?" Lorri asked.

Jim smiled broadly. "Some Christians have asked that same question! But seriously, denominations are very important. You need to think of them as associations of Christian churches which exist for the common good of the member churches. They perform very real functions, like providing pastors for vacant churches, pooling resources for mission projects, establishing seminaries and Bible colleges, and exercising discipline if pastors or teachers fall into sin or doctrinal error.

"I'm not suggesting there are *no* differences, but by and large the doctrinal differences among evangelical churches are minimal," Jim explained. "We have a saying in my particular fellowship: 'In essentials, unity; in nonessentials, liberty; in all things, charity.'

"The amazing thing is that the Bible speaks consistently to people in every tongue and century. In Africa you will find Christian brothers who believe what we call 'orthodoxy,' which is the very same body of Christian thought preached since the foundation of the church.

"And I might add that the Bible is full of warnings that false prophets would arise, teaching 'doctrines of devils.' Historically, those doctrines usually have centered upon the nature of God. And from what I've heard, Joseph Smith, whether knowingly or unknowingly, got caught up in doctrinal error. But you know what? We got off our discussion of the nature of God. Can we return to that?"

"Sure. But you're not saying you believe that Joseph Smith was a false prophet, are you?" Lorri asked with obvious worry in her voice. "I mean, the Church does so much good..."

"I don't want to be offensive, Lorri, but if Joseph taught what you say he did—and obviously he did—then I guess I would have to say he was deceived."

"And I don't want to be offensive either, Jim, but what makes *you* so smart?" she shot back.

"Wait a minute—we aren't talking about *me*," Jim insisted. "We're talking about orthodox Christianity. I'm not telling you that orthodoxy is right because *I* believe it. What you and I believe has no effect on truth. Truth exists independently of our opinion about it. But orthodoxy represents the doctrinal minimums which have remained firm in the church of Christ for 2000 years, in spite of frequent challenges from people like Joseph Smith.

"Basically, the Bible is a book about the relationship between God and man," he continued. "The central theme of the Bible is that in all the universe there is only one God. The Old Testament is the story of God calling the Jews back to the worship of the one true and living God. By the way, the belief in more than one God is called polytheism."

"Joseph Smith called it the plurality of Gods," Ted interrupted.

"Call it what you like, but the main thrust of the Bible is to call people from polytheism to monotheism—the belief in only one God."

"The Bible teaches the doctrine of many Gods," Ted said with determination.

"Please show me where."

Ted reached for his Bible and began flipping through the pages. "I'd be glad to."

Lorri smiled and said philosophically, "It must be a little discouraging to think that your destiny doesn't include Godhood."

Jim grinned and returned her smile. "I never thought I'd make a very good god. Besides, I'm absolutely convinced the position is filled!"

Lorri's smile broke into a wide grin as she laughed with Jim. "Oh, you character!" she cried good-naturedly.

Ted lifted his head from his search. "Here it is— 1 Corinthians 8:5. Listen to this:

> For though there be that are called *gods*, whether in heaven or in earth (as there be *gods* many and *lords* many) . . ."

Jim reached for Ted's Bible. "Can I see that?"

"Sure!" Ted responded with a grin, "Have a go at it!"

"You only read verse 5," Jim said as he peered over the page. "Let me read 4, 5, and 6:

> As concerning therefore the eating of those things that are offered in sacrifice unto idols, we know that an idol is nothing in the world, and that *there is none other God but one*. For though there be that are *called* gods, whether in heaven or in earth (as there be gods many and lords many), to us there is *but one God*, the Father, of whom are all things.

"You see," Jim protested, "this passage is *not* saying that there are many Gods. What it is saying is that there are many *demons*, and you can call them gods or lords if you want to, but in reality there is only one God."

Lorri felt a tight knot in her chest as her eyes met her husband's. "Ted, it does seem to say that."

Jim handed the Bible back and held it open for Ted to see. He reached over and picked up his own. "As long as we're looking at Scriptures, follow along and let me read a few other passages on this subject. Here is something from Isaiah, although I could go to almost any book in the Bible for this point. This is Isaiah 43:10,11:

> 'Ye are my witnesses,' saith the Lord, 'and my servant whom I have chosen, that

ye may know and believe me, and understand that I am he: Before me there was no God formed, neither shall there be after me. I, even I, am the Lord, and beside me there is no Saviour.'

"See, Ted and Lorri, God declares Himself to be the only God in the universe. Here's another passage in the next chapter, Isaiah 44:6:

Thus saith the Lord the King of Israel, and his redeemer, the Lord of hosts: 'I am the first and I am the last, and beside me there is no God.

"I mean, he says this over and over again. Here, look at verse 8:

Ye are even my witnesses: Is there a God beside me? Yea, there is no God; I know not any.

Both Ted and Lorri were listening intently. Jim ventured on. "The story is the same in the next chapter, in verses 5 and 6:

I am the Lord, and there is none else; there is no God beside me. . . . There is none beside me. I am the Lord, and there is none else.

Ted was frustrated. Jim was just not grasping this. "He is the God of *this* world," he explained, "just like his Father is the God of *his* world—*his* earth."

75

Jim looked at both Ted and Lorri and replied, "I don't think so, because He says right here in Isaiah 45:12:

I have made the earth and created man upon it. I, even my hands, have stretched out the *heavens*; and all their host have I commanded.

"The apostle John says that *this God* is the One who made *all things*, and that there wasn't *anything* made that *He* didn't make. The book of Job says that He binds and looses the constellations. Genesis says that in the beginning God made the *heavens* as well as the earth.

"The God of the Bible is the Creator. Nothing existed before He made it!" Jim exclaimed. "The Bible tells us that this God is all-powerful, all-knowing, and all-present."

There was color in Ted's cheeks as he felt anger rising in him. "Christians believe in more than one God too, Jim! Don't you believe in the Father, Son, and Holy Ghost?"

"Of course I do; I believe in the Holy Trinity. But the Trinity does not teach three Gods; it teaches one God who is Father, Son, and Holy Ghost."

"There's the double-talk again," Lorri muttered.

Jim ignored her and pressed on. "The Trinity is founded in our knowledge of the God of the Old Testament. Once we understand that there is only one God, then we understand that all His attributes—His power, knowledge, and presence—are expressed in three ways as Father, Son, and Holy Ghost."

Jim turned his attention back to Lorri. "Do you remember, Lorri, when Jesus said, 'Wherever two or three of you gather together in my name, there I am in the midst of you?' Is that familiar to you?"

"Yes, I remember," she responded cautiously.

"Well, we are gathered here right now attempting to know truth about God. Do you think Jesus is here?"

"I certainly do!"

"If there were a meeting at your church right now, do you think He would be there?" he continued.

Lorri became hesitant and sighed, "I suppose so."

Jim nodded his agreement. "Frankly, I believe if a prayer meeting is going on in China right now, Jesus is there too. Now that's all there is to the omnipresence of God. Jesus—who is God—is here."

"Well, what about Father? Heavenly Father certainly isn't here!" she cried out.

"Wait a minute." He raised his hand to calm her. "We said there is only one God. Remember what we just read in Isaiah? If Jesus is here, God is here."

"That's ridiculous!" she snapped. "God is God and Jesus is Jesus..."

Jim leaned back in his chair and pondered for a moment. "You know what I think the problem is here? Mormonism has not found the omnipotent, omniscient, omnipresent God. What Mormonism has found is a god you call an *exalted man*.

"If your God is big enough you won't have problems with how He expresses Himself, even if He does it in ways that are not fully comprehensible to you.

"You know, the nearest star to us is four light years away. It takes light *four years* to reach us from that star. That means if that star exploded tonight, we wouldn't know it for four years, because we couldn't possibly know it until the light reached here.

"But God is not like that. He is *throughout* His universe. Jesus—in the fourth chapter of John—said to the woman at the well that God is *spirit*. Do you want to hear something that will really stretch your thinking?"

Ted answered thoughtfully, "Yeah, sure, go ahead."

Lorri was skeptical. "I'm not sure *I* do."

Jim turned in his Bible as he continued. "Okay, I'm in the *third* chapter of John. This is Jesus talking to Nicodemus at night. Nicodemus is having trouble understanding about being born again. He thinks Jesus wants him to return to his mother's womb. Jesus chides him by saying:

> ... Art thou a master in Israel, and knowest not these things? ... If I have told you earthly things and ye believe not, how shall ye believe if I tell you of heavenly things?

"And then he tells him a *heavenly* thing:

> ... no man hath ascended up to heaven but he that came down from heaven, even the Son of man ...

"Now listen to this," Jim exclaimed, pointing to the page:

. . . which is in heaven.

"Since Jesus is God, He can, at one and the same moment, be in heaven while continuing to talk to Nicodemus in Jerusalem."

Ted reached for Jim's Bible. "Let me see that," he blurted out.

Ted and Lorri were not smiling. A look of fear crossed their eyes. They knew there was an answer for this, but it was outside their grasp. They looked at Jim with deep concern.

He looked at them and spoke from his heart. "Ted and Lorri, I really love you guys. And I know how committed to serving God you are. But I couldn't claim to love you if I didn't confront you with the fact that what your Church teaches is foreign to what the Old Testament prophets taught, what Jesus taught, and what the apostles taught.

"Tonight you've told me that as Mormons you believe God was once a man. You've said that Jesus was conceived through natural relations between Elohim, an exalted man, and the Virgin Mary. You've told me that you yourselves hope to become Gods.

"I must tell you that these are doctrines straight from the pit of hell. They didn't originate with Joseph Smith, either."

Ted jumped back as if hit physically by the words. "What do you mean?"

"Since you ask, I'll read it to you from the third chapter of Genesis:

Now the serpent was more subtle than any beast of the field which the Lord God had made. And he said unto the woman, 'Yea, hath God said, Ye shall not eat of every tree in the garden?' And the woman said unto the serpent, 'We may eat of the fruit of the trees of the garden; but of the fruit of the tree which is in the midst of the garden, God hath said, Ye shall not eat of it, neither shall ye touch it, lest ye die.' And the serpent said unto the woman, 'Ye shall not surely die, for God doth know that in the day ye eat thereof, then your eyes shall be opened, *and ye shall be as gods*, knowing good and evil.

"You see," Jim confided, "the *devil* is the originator of the doctrine that men may become Gods. Joseph was wrong.

"The Bible says, 'There is a way which *seems* right to a man, but the end thereof is destruction.' I know you believe that the Mormon Church possesses truth that the rest of Christendom has lost, but I'm convinced, after listening to your own profession of faith, that you have been deceived. That doesn't make you dishonest or evil—just *mistaken*.

"The problem is that being mistaken can cost you your soul," Jim explained. "You tell me you have a testimony that you are right—that Joseph Smith was a true prophet of God. And you seem to think that because six million Mormons believe it, somehow that makes it true. But I tell you that six *hundred* million Muslims believe that Islam is the one true religion and Mohammed its prophet. What we *believe* about something doesn't make it true. Your

burning in the bosom really doesn't prove anything. Joseph Smith's doctrines need to be judged
by the Bible, and nothing else, because no one can
come along and undo thousands of years of biblical
revelation with a vision.

"I have only one final Scripture that I want to
read. This is from a letter that Paul wrote to the
church at Rome. It's from the book of Romans, the
tenth chapter, the first four verses. Paul is writing
about the Jews—very religious people. He says:

> Brethren, my heart's desire and prayer to
> God for Israel is that they might be saved.
> For I bear them record that they have a zeal
> of God, but not according to knowledge.
> For they being ignorant of God's righ-
> teousness, and going about to establish
> their own righteousness, have not submit-
> ted themselves unto the righteousness of
> God. For Christ is the end of the law for
> righteousness to everyone that believeth.

Jim gently placed the Bible on the table and looked
up at his friends. "Ted and Lorri, you have submitted yourself to the laws and doctrines of Mormonism, but I'm afraid you haven't submitted yourself
to the righteousness from God. No matter how
many good things Mormonism may or may not
accomplish, if it leads people to worship a God
created in the image of man, it has done mankind a
great disservice.

"The Bible tells the story of the one true and
living God who made man. It tells us that man

separated himself from God through sin, and that today sin rages within the heart of man. It says that this same God 'took on flesh and dwelt among us'— that this mighty God allowed Himself to be crucified for the sins of all people who will receive Him as God and bend their knee to Him: confessing not that they will become Gods but that they already have become sinners, desiring not to *be* Gods but to *worship* the one true God, crying out in agony of spirit over their helpless condition and throwing themselves upon His wonderful mercy.

"Paul said that 'all have sinned and come short of the glory of God' and that all men are 'guilty before God.' He also said in the third chapter of Romans that 'by the deeds of the law there shall no flesh be justified,' but that we may be 'justified *freely* by his grace through the redemption that is in Christ Jesus.'

"Ted and Lorri, I know what I'm talking about. I was a very religious person, but I didn't know God. I went to church and worked day and night to be righteous, but I didn't know God. Then one day I met the real Jesus in simple faith. In an instant I was born again. I'm no longer trying to *become* acceptable to God; I *am* acceptable to Him—not through any righteousness of my own, but through the covering of His shed blood. I am one of those who was far away, although religious, but who has been made near in Christ."

Jim looked from Lorri to Ted and softly spoke from the depths of his heart. "Jesus is here right now. He *is* God. He made you and He loves you. He asks that you trade your religion for His relationship. It's your decision."

Silence settled like a heavy cloud over the three at the table. Jim waited quietly as Ted stared at him across the table in some silent, opened-mouthed demonstration of disbelief, his eyes crinkled up, blazing with hostility.

Lorri closed her eyes and held her head in her hands as she struggled to respond. "No! No! No!" she finally burst out, her voice cracking in pain. "You can't just drop that on us like that! It's *too* simple, *too* easy. How dare you? You have no right to say that to us!"

"It's not that easy, Lorri," Jim responded gently. "If it were, you both could do that right now without any jeopardy to your faith. But I'm afraid that such a step of faith in Christ being the full sin covering for your sins takes you beyond yourselves, beyond your own righteousness, beyond your own priesthood and your own godhood. That's why you're so upset right now.

"Ted. Look at me," he commanded as he turned back and forced Ted to make eye contact with him. "You *know* you will never be righteous enough in your own right. You *know* you lose that battle every day. And you *are* going to bow your knee to Christ. The Bible says in Philippians 2:10,11 that at His name *every* knee will bow and *every* tongue will confess that Jesus Christ is Lord! You are going to do it one day—either now or at that Great White Throne Judgment of those dead who are *not* in Christ, that judgment of the damned.

"I'm not talking about that Jesus who is your elder brother, or the Jesus who is the brother of Lucifer, or the Jesus who was appointed by some council of gods, but the Jesus who was and is fully God from before time began and who became flesh and shed His blood to pay the penalty for your sin. *That* Jesus is the true Christ. *That* Jesus stands at the door and knocks. He is waiting for you. He knows you by your name. He knows the number of hairs on your head and the number of your days, and He understands the deepest burdens of your heart."

Ted spread his hands out slowly on the table, breaking his gaze away from Jim's eyes to stare at his own hands. "I'm pretty confused here, Jim. I feel like I'm strangling. I can hardly breathe. I know the Church is true. I know Joseph Smith was a true prophet and the Book of Mormon is the—"

"Stop!" Jim cried out. "No one is challenging that! *I'm just talking about Jesus.* How could that possibly cause this kind of reaction, even if your Church were true, as you say it is?"

Ted stood abruptly and pushed his way past Lorri. Fighting his way from the kitchen, he made his way to the television and leaned down, removing the video from the VCR. "Here, please take this thing out of my house. I think we've gone beyond what I had hoped for." He shook his head slowly, his face flushed.

Both Jim and Lorri had followed him to the living room. Lorri held her eyes riveted to her husband, her face white, while Jim slowly walked across the room, accepting the video in the outstretched hand.

"I'll be glad to take it with me, Ted, but before I leave, something you said a while ago may help us through a very awkward farewell. Do you remember saying, 'As I see it, one of us is right and one of us is wrong'?"

"I certainly do remember, and I believe it even more strongly now that we have had this discussion," Ted acknowledged, still looking extremely uncomfortable.

"Well, how do we handle it, then? I think you can now understand my own concern for you, and with your help tonight I have gained a far deeper understanding of your concern for me!

"If we were all to die tonight, how could our grasp of heaven's promises have been enhanced by this time together? You see," he continued, "if the basic beliefs we hold are not common enough to bring all three of us into God's presence, then one of us is *truly* wrong and only the other right, as you said.

"Can't we all three ask for spiritual understanding, that same James 1:5 wisdom you say Joseph Smith asked for in the grove? Since we can't seem to agree on who that one true God is, can't we pray to Him in that way, knowing that He will hear and will answer and help the one who is wrong?" Jim looked to Ted and then Lorri, his eyes searching for that key to understanding.

Lorri spoke first, quietly asking, "Ted, that is all right, isn't it? I mean, we *can* pray together, can't we? Jim is seeking truth just as we have had to ourselves."

Ted relaxed visibly, a warm smile drew his wife to his side, and his grin broke into a hearty, genuine laugh. "Boy, I feel like I'm back on my mission. I haven't felt this kind of pressure since I had to go out and do this kind of stuff every day. Believe me, I'm ready to call it a day.

"You really are a good friend and an honest seeker of truth, Jim. Perhaps we should all chew on these things for a few days, and if you still have questions about the Gospel, we can get back again." He was back in control of things again. The pounding in his chest had stopped and he felt a wave of warmth throughout his being. That was the difference, he thought. Jim doesn't know about the power of the priesthood, the strength that one has from it, the confidence that all will be okay in the end.

But Jim wasn't going to be put off to some other discussion. He knew that it was time to go directly to the source of truth, since Ted and Lorri were as open right now as they would ever be. Tossing the tape on the chair behind him, he stepped over to the couple as they stood together in the center of the room. Placing a hand on the shoulder of each of them and without further consent, he began to pray. They both immediately dropped their heads in response.

"Father God," he petitioned, "You have observed us here tonight, seeking truth and understanding. We have realized that we have confusion here regarding Your very nature, Your very being. We pray to You, the one true God, above all other gods, in the name of Your one true Son, Jesus Christ, that You reveal Yourself to us, through Your truth, through Your Word, and through whatever form of personal revelation You choose, that whoever of us is in error, it will be made manifest, so that we may live in the light of Your truth. We three make ourselves available to Your instruction and pray this in the name of Your one true Son, Jesus Christ. Amen."

Ted and Lorri both sighed deeply and echoed a simultaneous "Amen." Lorri smiled broadly and picked up the videotape from the chair. "You weren't trying to leave this thing behind, were you?" she mugged in mock repulsion.

"No," Jim laughed. "I don't think it would get as much use here as it will in the church library. That is, unless you want it to take to your church tomorrow morning."

"We'll pass on that offer," Ted replied lightly. "I still have to prepare my Gospel Doctrine lesson for Sunday School, and it won't be your video."

The evening was over and the conversation turned to neighborhood things as they worked their way to the door and said their goodbyes.

6

SEARCHING FOR ANSWERS

Ted sat at the desk, working at his Sunday School lesson, as Lorri prepared for bed. His eyes wandered across the papers on his desk to his wife combing out her hair at the dressing table. He could tell that she was troubled. This had not been the easiest of nights. He doubted that Lorri had ever had her faith challenged as severely as it had been today. At least he himself had gone through it often enough while on his mission to know how to put his doubts behind him and trust in the Church and the Prophet.

"Oh, these darned knots!" she cried as she yanked impatiently at the brush. "I swear I'm going to get my hair cut short again and put an end to . . ." Lorri's voice trailed off. Putting her head in her hands, she began to sob. "I just don't know what to think anymore, Ted," she cried through her tears.

He laid aside the manual and gazed intently at his wife. "About what? About tonight, the Church, about Jim, about me? You don't know about what, honey?"

"About any of it! I'm completely confused. If Jesus *is* the head of the Church and a member of our Godhead, why did we both get so defensive every time Jim Stamper mentioned his name?" she replied in little bursts between the quieting sobs. "Don't you ever have doubts?"

"I don't allow myself to doubt!" he responded. "I guess we were upset because he tried to make faith in Jesus the center of our own personal salvation, not what we do with our faith. Without the teachings of our prophets and the instruction we have had in the Temple, we might have to settle for such a blind faith, but we know better, Lorri. We know what we have in store for us if we strive for perfection and endure to the end."

Lorri gave in to an immense sigh and slumped over onto the bed. "I'll never be a goddess," she muttered into the pillow. Turning to face her husband, Lorri brought something up from the deepest part of her doubts, something she had never dared to express before.

"I still don't understand how some of the things we did in the Temple are all that pleasing to God. I cringe every time I go through the Washing and Anointing Room," she said with obvious revulsion, "and I feel something terribly wrong at times when I embrace the worker representing Heavenly Father at the veil." She inhaled sharply as she verbalized the last of her inner secret.

"What on earth are you talking about? What could you possibly feel that's so terribly wrong?" Ted whispered.

"I feel something, sometimes," she stammered. "Sometimes when we put our arms through the slits and embrace, he pulls himself against me... too... tightly."

Ted leaned back in his chair and stared at the ceiling, rubbing the palms of his hands against his temples, pushing back against the throbbing pressure. "We are not supposed to talk about things that go on in the Temple. That's a sacred oath."

He sat back sharply, leaning over the desk toward his wife. "When did this first happen? What else don't you like about the Temple?"

"Ted, it happened the very first time, at the Provo Temple, when we were married. I was just too scared to talk about it. It only happens once in a while. I... just..." Lorri groped for the words, "feel sometimes in the Temple like I'm in some sort of foolish dress-up game that someone invented to make us look ridiculous. I just can't believe that Jesus dressed up that way or swore any oath of consecration or obedience to the Priesthood or the Prophet. It really *is* secret, Ted and I wonder just how *sacred* it really is."

"Lorri, your mother and dad went through the same ritual and so did their parents before them," Ted argued. "Your own mother was right at your side when you went through the veil when we were sealed. Are you saying that she would ever lead you into something that was bad for you?"

"That's unfair and you know it, Ted!" Lorri shot back harshly. "My mother was every bit a product of her own upbringing. What other choice did she have, living her whole life in the shadows of the Mormon Church? As a matter of fact, my mother *did* try to tell me . . . she did try to warn me, but I didn't understand it. She *hated* wearing her Temple garments, but wore them anyway, like obedient Mormon wives are supposed to."

Ted thought back to the first time he stood in front of a mirror, realizing that he was going to be wearing those things under his clothes for the rest of his life and then shuddering at the despair he felt as a young man used to working in the yard dressed in gym shorts and sandals. No wonder the brethren caution couples against talking about the Temple rituals.

Lorri's voice brought him back to the present dilemma. "Maybe you're comfortable in those things, Ted, but I have to tell you that there are days I want to rip this thing off my body. They're ugly and they make me ugly too!" She began sobbing again.

Ted looked mournfully at his lesson manual and rose from the desk. In two strong steps he was at her side and holding her in his arms. He silently stroked her head until the sobbing ceased and her breathing became measured and calm. Even in his silence, Lorri knew he understood her fears. In a way she was pleased. At least he didn't laugh at her or argue with what she shared.

Hours later, as Lorri slept peacefully by his side,

Ted lay awake, staring into space, working his way in frustration through the events of the night.

— ✦ —

In the frantic Sunday-morning race for church, Lorri and Ted barely had time to say hello. As one of the Counselors to the Bishop, he had rushed ahead for the Bishopric meeting scheduled before the early priesthood meeting. Lorri and the kids would come to church on their own. He was glad to get out of the house without talking about last night, and he hoped the Sunday services would help to get them back on track. Too bad there wasn't a Testimony meeting today. They always lifted Lorri's spirits.

The Bishop, the Ward Clerk, and the other Counselor were already in the office when Ted arrived. Within minutes they were caught up in the administration of the daily affairs of the Ward while Ted's thoughts kept wandering back to snatches of the video. He couldn't shake the images from his mind.

As the meeting worked its way to a finish, the Bishop closed the notebook that was his constant companion and waited quietly until he had the eye of each of them. "Brothers, we lost a family to the anti-Mormons this weekend," he spoke in almost a whisper. "The Bensons went to the film with her mother and have become born-agains. He called me last night to ask that their names be removed from the records of the Church. Ted, I'd like you to go over there with me and try to straighten them out before we have to go through with another excommunication."

Ted just couldn't believe his ears. The Bensons were a great young couple and Lorri was really close to Sister Benson. They were just working on a Stake Primary project together. "I can't, Bishop. I just can't. They were at my house for dinner only a week ago. We're too close for this kind of thing." Ted was feeling a panic rising up within him.

The Bishop's face lost its softness, and he acknowledged Ted's response with a curt nod. "Yes, you will, Brother Lindsey. I want you there *because* you are close. You're the one who got him his job last fall. You're the one who wanted him on your welfare project, and you're the one whose class he attends every week. He owes you a lot and will listen to you. You have to go, whether you like it or not. It is a responsibility of your calling. I *cannot* handle this without your help. I'll pick you up at six." He rose from his desk and walked from the room, ending the meeting without even a word of prayer.

Ted fumbled through his class, asking several members to read portions of the lesson and letting them ramble on at will. Lorri kept flashing some sort of warning signal with her eyes and pushed her way up to him as the class ended. "Ted, you're not going to believe this," she gasped. "Sister Benson called..."

"Hush this second, Lorri!" he hissed under his breath. "I know all about it. I'm supposed to go there tonight with the Bishop. Don't say a word to anyone."

Lorri stepped back in bewilderment. For the first time since the night before, she laughed. "I can't believe you knew about it already," she cried. "I get the scoop of the year and you're there ahead of me."

He reached out and squeezed her hand. "Only because Brother Benson called the Bishop last night." Ted put his hand on Lorri's shoulder and guided her toward the back hallway as the crowd of people moved around them toward the sanctuary as the Sacrament meeting began on the heels of Sunday School. "What did she say?"

Lorri had the twinkling look of a conspirator. "She said that she and Steve went to the movie with her mother and spent most of yesterday talking things over. They have been going through Temple preparation classes and had a lot of unanswered questions that they had been afraid to discuss. I guess they decided *it really is that easy*.

"Ted, they want to talk to us this afternoon. Steve really looks up to you. He needs to talk to someone he can trust. I invited them over for a barbecue. You and the Bishop can meet with them at our house." She smiled as she stared into his eyes. "Maybe we should invite Jim over, too."

Ted stared back at her in a state of confusion. "You're a changed woman from the lady I went to bed with last night, Lorri. What's different? I would expect you to be close to hysteria over the Bensons."

Lorri knew what was different. She felt like some pressure had been lifted off her spirit somehow last night. She felt refreshed and lighthearted this morning. Even when Sister Benson called, she was at peace.

"I guess it was finding out that I could have doubts and fears and you could understand and still love me deeply, without putting me down, Ted. I found out I could trust you all the way," she said softly, her face close to his. "It didn't resolve much of my dilemma, but it did strengthen my love for you."

Ted took her face into his hands. "I don't know what kind of day we have coming. I barely survived last night and you may have to shovel me into bed before this is all through. I *will* ask Jim to come over and share some of his thoughts with the Bishop, though. It should be quite a time."

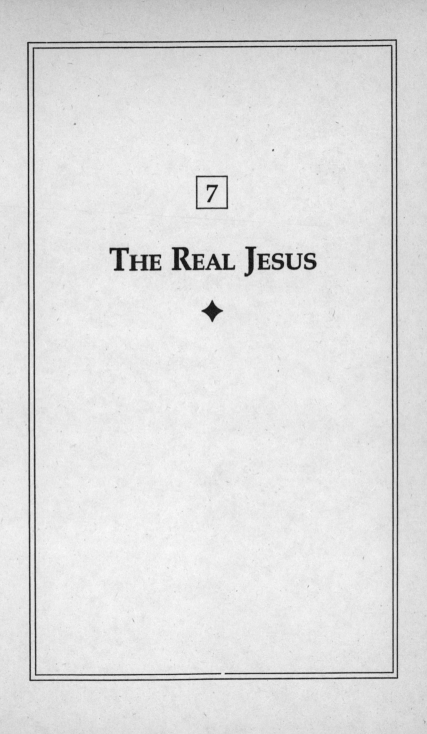

7

THE REAL JESUS

✦

S teve and Carol Benson's van turned into the Lindsey driveway and came to a stop. Steve slumped down in his seat as the two boys tore out of the car and around the corner of the house toward the back. Carol's eyes were riveted on her husband's face, searching out his eyes.

"I'd rather have my head amputated than to go through with this, Carol," he said softly, with just the edge of a grin working its way into the corners of his mouth. He rolled his head toward her and locked his eyes on hers. "Here we are, about to drop the bombshell of the year on our best friends, and in true Mormon style you've brought a casserole."

His grin broke out and joined her laughter as he reached over and kissed her firmly on the forehead. Carol was still laughing as she led the way around the house carrying her casserole like a trophy onto the patio. Lorri and Ted were already involved with separating several of the more energetic of the kids, and looked up in mock desperation at their friends.

"Finally, backup troops have arrived to save us from this horde," Lorri shouted with glee as she turned one squealing little boy upside down and lowered him gently to the grass, where he instantly scampered away, chasing after the alleged horde which was now making its way around the house. Lorri took Carol's proffered casserole and placed it with appropriate honors on the table, already loaded with food. "I'm so glad you came, Carol," she continued lightly. "I want to hear every single thing that happened!"

Ted and Steve had stepped back from the skirmish and greeted each other with a wary handshake, wisely leaving the opening remarks to their wives. Ted had become more than a little distressed while they sat waiting for the Bensons. The Bishop wasn't thrilled with the announcement that the Bensons were going to be at their house, and heaven only knew what he was going to do when he found Jim Stamper there too. Even that hadn't gone too well, since Jim was obviously ill at ease with the invitation. Ted had had to pry an acceptance out of him and then spent an hour in misery wondering why they wanted him there in the first place.

Now seeing that Steve was equally uncomfortable, he was able to smile warmly at his friend and relax. "I've been like a coiled spring all day, Steve," he confided privately. "I've been feeling like the anti-Mormons have stolen your soul away and I've been unable to fight for you. I'm *really* glad you came. I just pray that I can help. I never even dreamed you were losing your testimony."

Carol and Lorri had stopped their chatter and were watching the two men with great intent. "I never *lost* my testimony, Ted," Steve replied softly as he returned the smile. "We were searching for God's intent for our lives before we became Mormons and while we were Mormons, and I have to tell you, it got pretty confusing. The other night a lot of pieces fell into place and the answer ended up pretty simple after all."

Lorri stepped over to the two and put her hands on her hips in her best scolding posture. "Look, you guys are over here whispering and we can't talk and listen at the same time. This has to be one conversation and only one conversation," she demanded. While she spoke with a festive bravado, Ted knew Lorri was deeply serious that they not get divided into separate discussions, as was their usual practice. He saw the wisdom in her words.

"Let's all sit down and talk, then," Ted said as he motioned toward the table. "Lorri and I want you to tell us what happened this weekend. We are *truly* in deep shock." He stopped and studied the Bensons. *"What on earth happened?"*

Carol took Steve's hand as they sat before their friends and gripped it tightly. "My mom asked us to go see that film they showed at Christian Center," she began. "I was raised in the Baptist church, but by the time Steve and I were married, I had pretty much stopped going." She looked at Steve and then back to Lorri. "When the boys came, I knew we needed to get back into church, but the time never seemed right. When the Missionaries came to our house, I felt like it was an answer to our prayers. I told Steve that God knew our needs and sent them to us."

Carol stopped and caught her breath. "Everything happened so quickly, and when I told my mom that we were going to be baptized, she really came unglued and said a lot of terrible things about the Mormon Church!"

"Yet we met you two, and everyone in the Ward was so wonderful that I couldn't understand what was wrong with her. I thought, 'Well if you want to be that way, just be that way.'

"Things were pretty strained for awhile," she continued, "but my mom and I have always been good friends, so we just ended up agreeing not to agree about religion. Yet there was always that wall. I wanted so much for her to become a Mormon. She would have been such a tremendous Mormon.

"Last month she came over and told us that if we would do one thing with her, she would never bring up the subject of religion again. I could tell that she was really under a great deal of stress." Carol was struggling to smile. "So when we agreed, we found out that it was to go and see that film." Her gaze slowly dropped to the table and she fell silent.

Steve leaned forward and looked from Lorri to Ted. "That's where I came in. In the midst of all our objections about her methods and the movie, I knew that I *wanted* to see the film! I *wanted* to listen to that guy! I have to tell you, Ted, I've been having a lot of doubts lately. A lot of honest questions have been going unanswered around here and I've been feeling that if we have all this truth we always talk about, it shouldn't be that difficult to get some answers."

"You never came to me and told me you were having problems. You never went away from me with questions unanswered," Ted complained sharply.

"I'm sorry, Ted, but I *did* come to you more than once, but you always had some quick response that was the textbook reply for each occasion. When I asked you about this business of me becoming some polygamous God, you told me to wait until we had been through the Temple. You said that we would have a clearer understanding of our destiny, even though I told you that our need was more immediate.

"I didn't want to share my eternal life with other women, and Carol sure didn't want for the kids and her to have to share me with a bunch of other wives and kids. It was like you had this big secret, but just being good Mormons, we still weren't good enough yet to share it." Steve's voice had risen, and the kids were beginning to notice that the picnic was taking on a more serious tone. "I'm not upset about that, Ted. It was just real frustrating trying to study things out for myself at times. You were *never* the problem," he quickly assured his frowning friend.

"Let's toss the ball around with the kids," Steve bellowed as he scooped up a nearby volleyball and ran into the yard. Ted smiled plaintively at Lorri and lumbered slowly after him.

"This must be so hard for you, Carol," Lorri cried, reaching across to comfort her friend. She was devastated by the intensity of the emotions she had felt as they had spoken. "Ted was right, you know. These things all do become clear when you go through the Temple."

"Look, Lorri. I've had the same frustrations when you and I have talked about some of the same things. You haven't always been honest with me or yourself. Every time we've talked about the Temple, I've come away with two different stories from you. The first is what you say and the second is something down deep inside you, what I see in your eyes. They're not the same."

Lorri sat back stunned. Her thoughts flashed back to the look in her mother's eyes as she shared about the secrets of the Temple and the duties of a faithful Mormon wife. "Oh, dear God," she thought, "I'm just like my mother. I've been doing the same thing to Carol that my mother did to me." She heard Carol's voice droning on in the distance, but Lorri was consumed with the image of her mother sitting on her bed, attempting to reassure her that it was God's holiest purpose that she go through the Temple and take out her endowments so she could properly fulfill her divine role. She could still see that look of futility in her mother's eyes.

"... the rest of the food and I'll get the men to start the burgers going," Carol was saying as she rose from the table. Something had happened just then, and Carol knew it was time to drop the discussion. She had opened up a door that had deeply disturbed Lorri.

Lorri shook the thoughts away and busily began to set out the platters. "Ted, please go and get Jim and let Steve start the burgers. There are some hot dogs for the little kids.

"Josh!" she yelled at a small culprit dragging away a bag of chips. "Put that back right now!"

Tensions eased as they prepared the meal, and they were soon laughing again at Steve's droll humor as he entertained the kids with his outrageous efforts at the grill. Ted returned with an awkward Jim Stamper in tow, and they were soon relaxing over a great meal.

The kids had finished and wandered down to the street with their skateboards, bikes, and other weapons of transportation. The women were closing up the food platters and Jim Stamper was wandering back from his house sipping the spillage from a large, brimming cup of hot coffee.

"You Mormons missed the boat with this one," Jim laughed. "He who controls the coffeepot controls the world!" The other four booed and hissed with fitting disdain.

"Ted tells me that you were at Christian Center the other night," Jim smiled at the Bensons. "What did you think of the experience?"

"Well, you know we went there as Mormons prepared for the worst, Jim," Steve replied, "but we left in a totally different state of mind. Our eyes were really opened to a lot of things that had been troubling us for some time."

"That film was filled with a lot of lies and misrepresentations of our faith by a man filled with hate!" Ted cried out defensively.

Steve smiled sadly at the remark. His friend was so intent on defending the faith, even from a film he had never seen and a man he had never met. Instead of arguing, Steve turned to Carol. "What impressed you most about the evening, honey?"

"The film was every bit the bombshell it was advertised as. I thought the animation portion clearly put all the pieces together properly for the first time, though."

Jim glanced up and watched as Ted and Lorri locked eyes. A little smile broke out as he responded, "I thought so too. It may have been a little sensational in its approach, but it clearly defined basic Mormonism to me." His twinkling eyes innocently met those of Ted and Lorri before he looked back to Steve.

"What really opened my eyes was the question-and-answer time afterward," Steve said as he turned to Ted and Lorri. "Did you know that the Bishop was at the meeting?"

"*What are you saying?*" cried Lorri. "You *can't* mean that! What happened?" Ted was stunned at the news. The Bishop had never mentioned it, even to his counselors at the Bishopric meeting.

"At the end of the movie he was the very first to stand at the question-and-answer period. I didn't even see him until then. *I mean we almost died,*" Carol exclaimed. "He said that the film was nothing but a filthy pack of lies and if the people wanted to know about Mormonism they should ask a Mormon, a decent person, not someone excommunicated for failing to live the Gospel."

"I thought it was all over for the speaker, Ed Decker. You could hear a pin drop," Steve added. "But he just smiled and asked the Bishop what lies he was referring to and the Bishop said, '*All of them*.' He asked him again to be a bit more specific and again the Bishop said, '*All of them*.'

"The speaker said that the Bishop should pick his 'very best lie' from the movie and that he would document it right then completely from Mormon documents or fold his tent and leave town. He said, '*If I'm a liar, call my bluff right here in front of the whole town and I'll be out of business*.' But the Bishop just stood there. He couldn't name one single lie in the whole movie! It was then that some scales fell from my own eyes. It was like we have been playing games with God. Like I said before, if what we have is truth, what should we fear from any man?

"He started to call on someone down front, but the Bishop shouted out that the parts about the Temple ritual were all lies. Then Decker asked him if he had ever sworn blood oaths like we saw in the film and the Bishop shouted '*Never!*' Decker said that when he was a Mormon in the Temple, he had done so. He asked the Bishop, '*Did you put your thumb across your throat and swear an oath dealing with having your throat slit from ear to ear?*' The Bishop shook his fist at him and ran from the meeting. I mean he *ran out the door*. I couldn't believe my eyes. I mean it was like the Bishop was the liar!

"We sat there for over an hour while Decker fielded every question thrown at him. He had the answers; he did his homework. The guy probably knows Mormonism better than anyone I ever met," Steve continued. "But you know what I saw? He never ridiculed us or said these things to mock us.

Every time he gave the Mormon doctrine, he compared it with the orthodox biblical doctrine, and I began to see that the Gospel of Christ was really simple and clear, without all these frills that have had us so bogged down."

Carol had difficulty speaking, but slowly she sobbed out the rest. "It was what he said about the crosses being missing in our church buildings. He said that people who want to be their own gods can't deal with the cross and the blood shed at Calvary on our behalf. He talked about the water we use for sacrament—that it washes away the reality of Christ's shed blood."

She was silent for a moment, gathering her words carefully. "I looked behind him at the cross on the wall and knew what was missing in my life. I took one look at my mom and we both began to cry. At the end of the meeting, when the pastor had an altar call, *Steve and I went forward and gave our lives to the real Jesus.* Not the one who is the brother of Lucifer, not our Elder Brother, but Jesus who was God become flesh for us." Both Steve and Carol's faces were wet with tears as they relived the emotion of their experience.

Jim sat quietly in the background and listened as the Bensons continued to pour out their hearts to Lorri and Ted. Tears had begun to stream down Lorri's face and he could see the tiny quivers darting across the face of Ted as the Holy Spirit began to break through the wall of his heart.

He thought on the wonderful and perfect steps of the Lord and how He had brought these two people to such a place at such a time to be His ambassadors to this other couple whom He loved and for whom He died. "I could never have touched their hearts this way," Jim mused as he began to silently intercede for Ted and Lorri. He rose and walked into the house, leaving the friends alone to touch each other.

He was leaning against the kitchen counter, sipping on his now-cold coffee, when the phone rang. Jumping at the sound, Jim grabbed the phone as though it were an intruder breaking into the special things of God taking place outside. "Ted," barked the unseen voice, "this is the Bishop!" The voice sputtered over Jim's attempts to correctly identify himself. "I have *absolutely* no intention of meeting with those apostates. Tell them that their names will be off our records as quickly as I can act on it . . . and Ted, if you know what's good for you and Lorri, you better get them off your property and out of your lives . . . for good!" The phone went dead as Jim stared at it in amazement.

"Who was that?" called Lorri from the patio.

"Just the Bishop," Jim smiled broadly. "He called to say that he won't be able to make it tonight."

APPENDICES

NOTES

1. Jeremiah 1:5 KJV.
2. Bruce R. McConkie, *Mormon Doctrine*, 2nd ed. (Salt Lake City: Bookcraft, 1966), p. 322.
3. *Achieving Celestial Marriage (ACMM)*, Manual No. CDFR 60/61 (Salt Lake City: The Church of Jesus Christ of Latter-day Saints, 1976), p. 129.
4. *Pearl of Great Price (PGP)*, Book of Moses 3:5-7 (Salt Lake City: The Church of Jesus Christ of Latter-day Saints, 1977).
5. *ACCM*, p. 3.
6. *ACCM*, p. 129-30.
7. *Mormon Doctrine*, p. 321.
8. *Doctrine and Covenants (D&C)*, section 132 (Salt Lake City: The Church of Jesus Christ of Latter-day Saints, 1977).
9. *PGP*, Book of Abraham 3:23-28.
10. *Come Unto Christ*, Melchizedek Priesthood Manual (Salt Lake City: The Church of Jesus Christ of Latter-day Saints, 1984/1988), pp. 139-45.
11. *PGP*, Book of Abraham 3:28; Moses 4:1-3; *D&C* 29:36-37.
12. *PGP*, Book of Moses 5:16-41; 7:8-22.
13. *Mormon Doctrine*, pp. 526-27.
14. *ACCM*, p. 235.
15. *Mormon Doctrine*, pp. 546-47, 742.
16. McConkie speech, "All Are Alike Unto God."
17. *PGP*, J. Smith 2:19-20.
18. *Come Unto Christ*, pp. 139-45.
19. *ACCM*, pp. 131-32.
20. *History of the Church*, Vol. 6 (Salt Lake City: Deseret Book Co., 1967), pp. 408-09.

CREEDS OF CHRISTIANITY

The Apostles' Creed

I believe in God the Father Almighty, Maker of heaven and earth, and in Jesus Christ, His only Son, our Lord, who was conceived by the Holy Ghost; born of the Virgin Mary; suffered under Pontius Pilate; was crucified, dead, and buried; He descended into hell; the third day He rose again from the dead; He ascended into heaven and sits at the right hand of God the Father Almighty; from thence He shall come to judge the living and the dead.

I believe in the Holy Ghost, the holy Christian church, the communion of the saints, the forgiveness of sins, the resurrection of the body, and the life everlasting. Amen.

The Nicene Creed

I believe in one God, the Father Almighty, Maker of heaven and earth and of all things visible and invisible, and in one Lord Jesus Christ, the only-begotten of His Father before all worlds, God of God, Light of Light, Very God of Very God, Begotten, not made, being of one substance with the Father, by whom all things were made; who for us men and for our salvation came down from heaven and was incarnate by the Holy Ghost of the Virgin Mary and was made man; and was crucified also for us under Pontius Pilate.

He suffered and was buried; and the third day He rose again according to Scripture and ascended into heaven, and sits at the right hand of the Father; and He shall come again in glory to judge both the quick and the dead, whose kingdom shall have no end.

And I believe in the Holy Ghost, the Lord and Giver of life, who proceeds from the Father and the Son, who with the Father and the Son together is worshiped and glorified, who spoke by the prophets. And I believe in one holy Christian and apostolic church. I acknowledge one baptism unto the remission of sins, and I look for the resurrection of the dead and the life of the world to come. Amen.

LDS Support
Documentation

Nature of God

Achieving Celestial Marriage Manual (ACCM), 1976, page 129L/R

God was once a mortal man. He lived on a planet like our own. He experienced conditions similar to our own and advanced step by step.

Bruce R. McConkie, *Mormon Doctrine (MD), 1966, 322R*

"Further, as the Prophet also taught, there is "a god above the father of our Lord Jesus Christ. . . . If Jesus Christ was the son of God, and John discovered that God the Father of Jesus Christ had a father, you may suppose that he had a father also. Was there ever a son without a father?" (quoting Joseph Smith).

ACMM page 3

"What you are saying is that God became God by obedience to the Gospel program, which culminates in eternal marriage. Yes."

Doctrine and Covenants (D&C) 130:22

God has a body of flesh and bones as tangible as man's.

ACMM page 129L   God is now an exalted man with powers of eternal increase. He lives in an exalted Marriage relationship.

ACMM 129R, 130L   We are the literal Children of God, a part of his family unit. We lived with our heavenly parents before coming to earth.

ACMM page 4RL   ... giving birth to spirit children and setting them on the road to exaltation. And if this is to be done, you must have an exalted man and an exalted woman.

MD page 239L   God continues to progress, as his own creations expand and his spirit offspring multiply.

Preexistence and Our First Estate

Moses 3:5-7, *Pearl of Great Price (PGP)*   Every form of life was created spiritually in Kolob first.

Abraham 3:22,23 *PGP*   In the beginning we were all spirit children, living in the presence of God, our heavenly father.

Jesus the Christ, James Talmage, 1968, pages 15-16   James Talmage's detailed explanation of the primeval council of the Gods.

Abraham 3:23-28 *PGP*   Council called of all the leading spirits.

Abraham 4:25,26 *PGP*	God proposed a plan for our progression.
Abraham 3:24-26 *PGP*, *D&C* 29:39, John 16:28 KJV, Jeremiah 1:5 KJV	That plan was for us to come to earth, and gain physical bodies, to learn good from evil and to have the free agency to choose which path we each wanted to follow.
Moses 4:1-4 *PGP*, Abraham 3:27,28 *PGP*; Isaiah 14:12-17 KJV	Lucifer, our elder brother who desired glory, stood up and proposed his own plan.
Spencer W. Kimball, "Jesus of Nazareth," in *Ensign*, Dec. 1980 (First Presidency message), pages 3-5.	His trials were continuous. Perhaps his brother, Lucifer, had heard him say when he was still but a lad of 12, "Wist ye not that I must be about my Father's business?" (Luke 2:49). Then came the time when Satan thought to trip him. Their encounter in the previous world had been on more equal terms, but now Jesus was young and Satan was experienced.
Moses 4:1-3 *PGP*	Lucifer's plan was to take away our free agency, force us to obey all the law. He wanted us to worship him.

Moses 4:2 *PGP*	Jesus stood and offered himself as our sin offering, giving man his free agency and the chance to attain eternal glory, or godhood with heavenly father.
Abraham 3:28 *PGP*	All the council voted No to Lucifer and Yes to Jesus.
Abraham 3:28 *PGP*, *D&C* 29:36-37, Revelation 12:7-9	Lucifer, very angry, persuaded one third of the spirit children to follow him and rebel against God and the plan of Jesus. They were cast from God's presence and sent to this earth without bodies of flesh and blood.
MD page 828, *D&C* 29:36-41	Describes the war in heaven, Lucifer sent here where he continues to battle against the saints.
Moses 5:16-41 *PGP* *MD* pages 526-28 Moses 7:8-22 *PGP*	Those who were least valiant in preexistence are known in mortality as negroes. They came to earth through lineage of Cain, with black skins.

Creation of the Earth and Our Second Estate

D&C 77:12, Moses 1:39 *PGP*, Abraham 3:19 *PGP*	The earth was created, in the same fashion of many worlds, populated by intelligent people, in his image. Man would always be learning and growing.

Abraham 2:2-8 *PGP*	God tells Abraham about the control center, Kolob.
Moses 6:51-68 *PGP* Moses 3:17 *PGP* Genesis 3:4,5 KJV Moses 4:12,13 *PGP*	The Garden of Eden story. Tells of the many gods involved.
Private letter dated Feb. 19, 1981, page 6	Apostle Bruce R. McConkie to Mr. Eugene England at BYU: "Yes, President Young did teach that Adam was the father of our spirits, and all the related things that the cultists ascribe to him." McConkie then denies it is true, even though it is documented in church records.
2 Nephi 9:25,26 *Book of Mormon (BoM)*, tr. J. Smith (Herald House, 1973), Alma 42:17-21 *BoM*	The earth is controlled by laws. If we break one of them we must be punished.
Moses 4:29-31 *PGP*	Adam and Eve are cast out of the Garden.
Moses 5:6-9 *PGP*	They learn that their transgression was necessary that man might live. Adam is baptized, receives Holy Ghost and the priesthood. He becomes the first patriarch.

MD 546R-547L — Our Lord is the only Son of the Father in the flesh. Each word is to be understood literally.... Christ was begotten by an immortal father in the same way that mortal men are begotten by mortal fathers.

MD 742L — God is an immortal personage. Christ is his literal son. There is nothing figurative about his paternity. He was begotten, conceived and born in the normal and natural course of events.

ACMM page 235L — The Lord is now sending the Choicest Spirits to earth. "I see an improvement each few years in the young people of the Church. I believe that you are the cream of all the spirits in the hosts of heaven and God has sent you here to do a great work" (Mark E. Petersen, BYU address on February 3, 1953).

Godhood and Our Third Estate

MD 321L — That exaltation which the saints of all ages have so devoutly sought is Godhood itself.

MD 321R

You have got to learn how to be gods yourselves ... the same as all gods have done before you (quoting Joseph Smith).

History of Church, Vol. 6, page 306

My Father worked out His Kingdom with fear and trembling, and I must do the same; and when I get my kingdom, I shall present it to My Father, so that He may obtain Kingdom upon Kingdom, and it will exalt Him in glory. He will then take a higher exaltation, and I will take His place, and thereby become exalted myself.

ACMM page 3R

If God became God by obedience to all of the gospel law with the crowning point being the celestial law of marriage, then that's the only way I can become a god.

ACMM 203L

The endowment is the celestial course of instruction, being enabled to give them the key words, the signs and tokens, pertaining to the priesthood and gain your eternal exaltation in spite of earth and hell.

D&C 124:28-36 127:128 128:15ff.	Baptism for the dead: the keys to the holy priesthood ordained so you may receive honor and glory; for their salvation [the dead] is necessary and essential to our salvation.
D&C 131	Three degrees of glory with celestial the highest.
Moses 1:39 *PGP*	This is my work and my glory— to bring to pass the immortality and eternal life of man.
D&C 132:19,20	Then shall they be Gods, they shall have all power, the angels are subject to them.
MD 529R, 530L	Celestial Marriage is the new and everlasting covenant of marriage.
Newell and Avery, *Mormon Enigma*, (Doubleday, 1984)	Book relates the aversions that Emma Smith, Joseph's wife, had to the law of plurality of wives.

Joseph Smith

Come Unto Christ, pages 126-32	If we get our salvation, we shall have to pass by him; if we enter into our glory, it will be through the authority that he has received. We cannot get around him.

D&C 1:17,18 *D&C* 35:17	God called Joseph Smith and commanded him to proclaim the gospel. Fullness of gospel sent forth by JS.
History of the Church Vol. 6, pages 408-09	I have more to boast of than ever any man had. I am the only man that has ever been able to keep a whole church together since the days of Adam. ... Neither Paul, John, Peter, nor Jesus ever did it. I boast that no man ever did such a work as I.
Joseph Smith (JS) 2:30-59 *PGP*	The story, in Joseph's own words, of Moroni's visit, the uncovering of the gold plates, and the eventual translation of the Book of Mormon.
JS 2:55,56 *PGP*	Joseph involved in treasure-seeking.
JS 2:17-20 *PGP*	All Christian creeds were an abomination in his sight.
D&C 20:1,2	Joseph Smith commanded to organize the church.

Other Good Harvest House Reading

THE GOD MAKERS
by *Ed Decker* and *Dave Hunt*

This unique exposé on Mormonism is factual, carefully researched, and fully documented. *The God Makers* provides staggering new insights that go beyond the explosive film of the same title. An excellent tool in reaching Mormons.

ANSWERS TO THE CULTIST AT YOUR DOOR
by *Robert* and *Gretchen Passantino*

This book is for anyone who wants a basic understanding of the cults without undue research! Concise reviews and answers to the beliefs of Jehovah's Witnesses, Hare Krishnas, The Way International, Mormons, and Moonies. Highly recommended by Walter Martin.

WITNESSES OF JEHOVAH
A Shocking Exposé of What Jehovah's Witnesses Really Believe
by *Leonard* and *Marjorie Chretien*

Two ex-Jehovah's Witnesses candidly reveal the hidden facts about the Watchtower Society in order to expose this harmful pseudo-Christian organization for what it is.

THE CULT EXPLOSION
by *Dave Hunt*

This book exposes the real danger and the strategies employed by cults of our time. Must reading for anyone who wants to understand the subtle ways cults prey upon the fears and needs of so many people.

DEATH OF A GURU
by *Rabi Maharaj* with *Dave Hunt*

Descended from a long line of Brahmin priests and trained as a yogi, Rabindranath Maharaj becomes a great Hindu leader. His autobiography, written by bestselling author Dave Hunt, traces his difficult search for meaning, his increasing disillusionment, and his struggle to choose between Hinduism and Christ.

WHEN THE WORLD WILL BE AS ONE
The Coming New World Order in the New Age
by *Tal Brooke*

Today the pieces are falling into place for a worldwide transformation. In the not-too-distant future a New World Order, unlike anything the world has ever seen, could appear almost overnight. There is an emerging global consciousness that is either an incredible historical coincidence or is, in fact, part of a sophisticated plan whose beginnings can be traced to antiquity. Could this be the global reality predicted 2,000 years ago by a prophet on the Isle of Patmos?

Tal Brooke spent two decades intently exploring the occult. His quest ultimately landed him in the heart of India where for two years he was the top Western disciple of India's miracle-working superguru, Sai Baba. Tal is a graduate of the University of Virginia, and Princeton, and is a frequent speaker at Oxford and Cambridge universities.

Dear Reader:

We would appreciate hearing from you regarding this Harvest House nonfiction book. It will enable us to continue to give you the best in Christian publishing.

1. What most influenced you to purchase *The Mormon Dilemma*?
   - ☐ Author
   - ☐ Subject matter
   - ☐ Backcover copy
   - ☐ Recommendations
   - ☐ Cover/Title
   - ☐ _____

2. Where did you purchase this book?
   - ☐ Christian bookstore
   - ☐ General bookstore
   - ☐ Department store
   - ☐ Grocery store
   - ☐ Other

3. Your overall rating of this book:
   - ☐ Excellent ☐ Very good ☐ Good ☐ Fair ☐ Poor

4. How likely would you be to purchase other books by this author?
   - ☐ Very likely
   - ☐ Somewhat likely
   - ☐ Not very likely
   - ☐ Not at all

5. What types of books most interest you?
   (check all that apply)
   - ☐ Women's Books
   - ☐ Marriage Books
   - ☐ Current Issues
   - ☐ Self Help/Psychology
   - ☐ Bible Studies
   - ☐ Fiction
   - ☐ Biographies
   - ☐ Children's Books
   - ☐ Youth Books
   - ☐ Other _____

6. Please check the box next to your age group.
   - ☐ Under 18
   - ☐ 18-24
   - ☐ 25-34
   - ☐ 35-44
   - ☐ 45-54
   - ☐ 55 and over

Mail to: Editorial Director
Harvest House Publishers
1075 Arrowsmith
Eugene, OR 97402

Name _____

Address _____

City _____ State _____ Zip _____

Thank you for helping us to help you in future publications!